Challenges and Potential of a Collaborative Approach to Education Reform

Susan J. Bodilly

Joan Chun

Gina Ikemoto

Sue Stockly

Prepared for the Ford Foundation

 EDUCATION

The research described in this report was conducted by RAND Education for the Ford Foundation.

Library of Congress Cataloging-in-Publication Data

Challenges and potential of a collaborative approach to education reform / Susan Bodilly ... [et al.].
  p. cm.
  "MG-216."
  Includes bibliographical references.
  ISBN 0-8330-3652-1 (pbk.)
  1. School improvement programs—United States—Case studies. 2. Community and school—United States—Case studies. 3. Education, Urban—United States—Case studies. 4. Collaborating for Education Reform Initiative. I. Bodilly, Susan J. II. Rand Corporation.

LB2822.82.C397 2004
371.2'00973—dc22

                                                                    2004012847

The RAND Corporation is a nonprofit research organization providing objective analysis and effective solutions that address the challenges facing the public and private sectors around the world. RAND's publications do not necessarily reflect the opinions of its research clients and sponsors.

RAND® is a registered trademark.

Published 2004 by the RAND Corporation
1700 Main Street, P.O. Box 2138, Santa Monica, CA 90407-2138
1200 South Hayes Street, Arlington, VA 22202-5050
201 North Craig Street, Suite 202, Pittsburgh, PA 15213-1516
RAND URL: http://www.rand.org/
To order RAND documents or to obtain additional information, contact
Distribution Services: Telephone: (310) 451-7002;
Fax: (310) 451-6915; Email: order@rand.org

Preface

In 1997, the Ford Foundation began a new effort at school improvement called the Collaborating for Education Reform Initiative (CERI). It sent out a request for proposals to sites it was familiar with, asking them to create collaboratives of community-based organizations that would help create and sustain education reforms in their local areas. In all, the foundation selected eight sites to be a part of this effort and funded them for several years.

As part of this effort, the foundation sponsored a formative assessment of the sites' progress to be carried out by the RAND Corporation beginning in 1999. This monograph is the first public reporting on the effort and documents the progress of the sites from inception to spring of 2003.

The audiences for this report are policymakers involved in trying to build sustained support for educational improvement and practitioners interested in using collaborative efforts among community organizations to improve public educational services.

This research was conducted within RAND Education, under the direction of Dominic Brewer. This research effort reflects RAND Education's mission to bring accurate data and careful, objective analysis to the national debate on education policy.

The RAND Corporation Quality Assurance Process

Peer review is an integral part of all RAND research projects. Prior to publication, this document, as with all documents in the RAND monograph series, was subject to a quality assurance process to ensure that the research meets several standards, including the following: The problem is well formulated; the research approach is well designed and well executed; the data and assumptions are sound; the findings are useful and advance knowledge; the implications and recommendations follow logically from the findings and are explained thoroughly; the documentation is accurate, understandable, cogent, and temperate in tone; the research demonstrates understanding of related previous studies; and the research is relevant, objective, independent, and balanced. Peer review is conducted by research professionals who were not members of the project team.

RAND routinely reviews and refines its quality assurance process and also conducts periodic external and internal reviews of the quality of its body of work. For additional details regarding the RAND quality assurance process, visit

http://www.rand.org/standards/

Contents

Figures

Tables

Summary

This report documents a formative evaluation of an effort begun by the Ford Foundation to develop collaboratives in eight urban centers from fall 1999 to spring 2003. The effort continues to evolve today.

Collaborating for Education Reform Initiative

After years of attempting to improve education outcomes for all students and not seeing the fully desired results, the Ford Foundation had become frustrated with traditional approaches to reform. Through internal discussions and examination of other initiatives, the foundation staff became convinced that specific sites could make quality teaching in all classrooms a reality by employing a combination of tactics, such as effectively linking the different levels of pre-K–12 to higher-education systems; promoting informed public dialog, debate, and consensus-building around school reform options; promoting professional development for faculty, staff, and administrators; promoting district and state policy changes; and enhancing the role of parents and caregivers. This strategy for school improvement emphasized changing the organization and culture of schools, their relationships with their stakeholders, and the systems in which they are embedded. The Ford sponsors believed that the more coherent, steady, and coordinated these multiple approaches were, the more likely they were to succeed where other disjointed or discontinuous efforts had failed.

The Ford Foundation translated this belief into a strategy for reform: *local collaboration*. This philosophy grew out of, in part, sharing lessons from other foundations' experiences with collaborative efforts including the Annenberg Challenge Grants and the Pew Charitable Trust's Systemic Initiative. But, it was also a result of the Ford Foundation's own previous efforts at collaborative formation supported from 1991 to 2000 called the Urban Partnership Program (UPP).

Based on its own experiences with the UPP initiative and knowledge of other reform efforts, the Ford Foundation chose to encourage the development of collaboratives of community-based organizations in urban settings to address systemic barriers to high-quality teaching and learning. By basing the impetus for reform largely outside of the public school central office, the Ford Foundation hoped to avoid the pattern of failure of reforms that originated solely from the central office and were led by a "transformational," and often brief-tenured, superintendent. These internal efforts often dissipated when district leadership turned over. Ford envisioned collaboratives with multiple member organizations that could outlive the administrations of public officials. Furthermore, Ford hoped that collaborative supported reforms would also potentially avoid the failures associated with internally mandated reforms that are not supported by the community or by school personnel. By working from the outside inward and by involving school staff in planning and constructing the interventions, Ford sponsors hoped that buy-in and commitment to reform efforts would increase.

Thus the foundation began a new initiative, called the Collaborating for Education Reform Initiative (CERI), by issuing a series of planning grants in July 1999. As stated in the request for proposals (RFP), "system-wide reform efforts require effective coalitions among organizations which are committed to systemic educational reform over an extended period of time and who project their efforts to the state-level" (Ford Foundation, 1999, p. 1). In school years 1998–1999 and 1999–2000, it extended implementation grants to organizations in eight communities to begin implementation of CERI. These sites were Cataño P.R., Charlotte-Mecklenburg, N.C., Denver,

Colo., the District of Columbia, Jackson, Miss., Miami-Dade, Fla., San Antonio, Tex., and Santa Ana, Calif. As part of this effort, the foundation asked the developing collaboratives in these areas to work initially in a cluster of schools within the district—usually a feeder pattern of elementary schools, middle schools, and a high school. At the same time, Ford expressed its expectation that collaboratives would create systemic changes across the entire district.

The composition and focus of the eight collaboratives differed substantially. At the time the initial grants were awarded, the number of collaborative members ranged from five in one site to 19 in another and included local colleges and universities, community-based organizations, advocacy groups, educators, parents, and concerned citizens. By design, the award amounts of $300,000 per year were not intended to fund a districtwide reform effort. Rather, given the existence of community-based organizations in each setting that were interested in education improvement, the funds were intended to be used to unite community-based organizations and other organizations, such as the central office, in a way that could produce greater improvement and a stronger, more consistent focus on the reform agenda. As such, a major expected outcome was strong interorganizational linkages that enabled stronger implementation of the school improvement effort in a community.

RAND's Formative Evaluation

In fall 1999, RAND began a formative evaluation of the effort. The evaluation had three purposes: to provide feedback to sites to improve their efforts, to provide information to Ford to inform its decisions about support and funding provided to sites, and to document for the public the challenges and possible successes of this approach to improvement. The research questions were the following:

• Did sites show progress toward desired outcomes?

- Could lessons learned or promising practices be discerned from the experiences of individual collaboratives or the group as a whole?
- Could collaboratives be effectively created by such an outside influence as the Ford Foundation to sustain education improvement efforts?

This report describes RAND's findings concerning the progress made by those sites selected by the Ford Foundation and the lessons learned to date—i.e. four years into the effort to build collaboratives intended to sustain focused reform. The report should help other community organizations, policymakers, and those responsible for the education of our children to understand whether a collaborative approach to education reform might be useful in their communities.

Methodology

The foundation proposed an initiative that was context-specific—i.e., set in real-life communities. It did not impose a uniform set of interventions but rather expected collaboratives to create and implement interventions relevant to their goals and the needs of their communities. As such, CERI was a development effort suitable for a qualitative research approach that included descriptive analysis.

We chose an embedded case study approach, using mixed methods as appropriate for this challenge, and viewed each collaborative and its surrounding community as a single embedded case. To assess the individual and comparative progress of sites, we collected and analyzed multiple data sources including RAND-developed teacher and student surveys, extensive field interviews, documents, such as newspaper articles and printed materials provided by collaborative members, and quantitative data supplied by districts and schools.

During the course of the study, we, in conjunction with others involved in the initiative, developed and agreed to a set of five dimensions along which we would judge the progress made by individual sites in establishing well-functioning collaboratives that promote improved learning. These dimensions were based on a review of literature on collaboratives and the specific goals Ford had set out in supporting the formation of collaboratives. They included the following:

- The level of development of interorganizational linkages.
- The level of development and implementation of plans for providing high-quality teaching and learning in the cluster.
- The level of development and implementation of plans for systemic changes in policy.
- The level of independence achieved by the collaborative.
- The level of change in student outcomes as a result of collaborative actions.

Findings

We found that the CERI effort to date resulted in several functioning collaboratives as defined by the first four dimensions listed above. The latter dimension, change in student outcomes, could not be clearly demonstrated in many cases in part because of data limits and in part because of the lack of elapsed time. In answer to our first research question, the sites showed variable progress with regard to the different dimensions. The following points summarize the progress made.

- Dimension 1: All of the grantees developed networks to share information and to act cooperatively with each other. Four of the eight grantees, those in Cataño, D.C., Jackson, and Miami, made comparatively strong progress toward the formation of deeper organizational linkages as defined in the literature on collaboratives. San Antonio had difficulty operating jointly and crafting joint products, functioning cooperatively instead. The Santa Ana grantee created a well-functioning partnership to bring grant money into the area. Grantees in Denver and Charlotte made weaker progress in the development of organizational linkages.

- Dimension 2: Although never fully implementing all of their activities, four grantees contributed to the development and implementation of visions of high-quality teaching and support in their locales (Cataño, D.C., Jackson, Miami). The others, each with less-developed organizational linkages, made weaker progress toward implementation at least in part because members did not agree on the vision or did not pool their resources to implement it.

- Dimension 3: Three of the grantees, those in Cataño, D.C., and Jackson made progress toward policy changes and/or toward expanding policy influence. The collaborative in Miami-Dade did not see its work in terms of systemic change and did not move deliberately toward ensuring districtwide support of changes to policy. Four grantees—Charlotte, Denver, San Antonio, and Santa Ana—were at the planning stages of policy changes.

- Dimension 4: Cataño and D.C. took significant steps toward sustaining the collaborative and its CERI focus through a combination of opportunistic and deliberate actions. Santa Ana also took steps to bring in significant grant funding, but this was directed toward other initiatives. Others were in the planning stages or had perhaps drawn in some minor funding supports.

- Dimension 5: Very little improvement on student achievement that could be attributed to the grantees was evident across most sites. Jackson, Miami, and Santa Ana, however, might be credited with some test successes. Cataño might be credited with increasing the percentage of children staying in school through the middle school years. Test scores there, however, did not paint a consistent picture of progress.

In terms of lessons learned, we identified several factors that were responsible for the difference in progress across sites. Much of the difference in progress could be traced to the difficulties of creating collaboratives themselves. Our data revealed that, in combination with other factors, significant time and member interaction were necessary to build the levels of trust for collaboratives to function. Other factors that we found important to progress included the following:

- Inclusion of stakeholders integral to the local context and able to contribute to the collaborative's goals.
- The perceived legitimacy and authority of the lead organization.
- How collaborative members worked together.
- The characteristics of and action by the collaborative leadership.
- The fostering of the collaborative's legitimacy and reputation over time.
- The matching of goals to the local context.
- The adept use of data to inform theories of action and activities.
- The habit of continuously reflecting on work and the use of data to alter strategies as necessary.
- Early attention to a plan for institutionalizing systemic change, including strategies for sustaining the collaborative as well as sustaining and scaling-up the reform agenda.

While progress was made and some promising collaboratives have developed, none has reached the final outcomes that the funders desired. This, while disappointing, holds out some hope: that collaborative building, while a long and possibly arduous process, is one with some significant promise.

Observations on Improving Efforts at Collaborative Building

Further lessons from this effort point to actions that, in hindsight, the foundation could have conceivably controlled and that might have contributed to a slow start for some sites. We suggest that future efforts at collaborative formation provide for:

- Stronger planning and coordination among foundation staff.

- Clearer communication of expectations at the start of the initiative.
- Technical assistance in the use of data for diagnosis of problems, strategic planning, development of activities, and feedback, especially during the planning stages.
- More routine and regular convenings and data-sharing aimed at providing sites with opportunities to learn about progress generally and their progress compared to others.

In answer to our last research question, we conclude from all of the above that indeed collaboratives can be deliberately formed with support by outside funders, such as the Ford Foundation. However, it is not a certain process. Adopting the above suggestions cannot guarantee strong progress but might reduce the barriers to strong collaborative formation, such as those faced by the sites in this study.

Acknowledgments

We wish to thank the many people who contributed to this work.

The Ford Foundation program officers were a major source of inspiration and insight during the course of this project. Janice Petrovich, Cyrus Driver, Steven Zwerling, and Joe Aguerreberre from the foundation all provided guidance and support.

The project could not have been completed without the significant help of the members of each of the eight collaboratives studied, especially their leaders. In addition, schools involved with the collaboratives opened their doors to us to help study the impact of implemented activities. Districts provided us with significant support in terms of data and time. We thank all of them for their support and contributions.

Several members of the RAND staff contributed greatly to the work contained within this report. Ana Suarez, James Garluski, and Hilary Darilek were responsible for the survey work. R. J. Briggs and Hilary Darilek provided significant support in the collection and analysis of quantitative data. Irene Brahmakulam acted as a research assistant and aided in the fieldwork. Donna Boykin played a major role in setting up the site visits. Much of this report rests on their contributions.

Reviewers played an important role throughout this project. These included Sheila Kirby, Kerri Kerr, Julie Marsh, Amanda Datnow, and Victor Young. We thank them for their insights and efforts to make our work better. While they helped improve the report, the final contents are the responsibility solely of the authors.

Abbreviations

AMSJE	Alianza Metropolitana de San Juan Para La Educación (Puerto Rico)
CERI	Collaborating for Education Reform Initiative
CMS	Charlotte-Mecklenburg School District
CSAP	Colorado Student Assessment Program
DCPS	District of Columbia Public Schools
DEN	Denver Education Network
FCAT	Florida Comprehensive Assessment Test
FRL	Free and Reduced-Price Lunch (program)
GED	General Education Development (diploma)
JPS	Jackson Public School (district)
LCN	Learning Communities Network
LEP	Limited English Proficiency
NECA	Network for Educators on the Americas
PEBC	Public Education and Business Coalition
PPS	Parents for Public Schools
RFP	Request for Proposal
SY	School Year
UPP	Urban Partnership Program

CHAPTER ONE

Introduction

In the 1980s and 1990s, several realities concerning K–12 education became increasingly clear. First, failures in the performance of the public system were not pervasive but were particularly centered in our urban and rural areas populated by low-income and less-educated families. Second, the federal and state governments began what has become known as the standards and accountability movement in an attempt to ensure that all students met high standards of performance. Third, improving student performance required improving the quality of teachers and teaching in our lowest-performing schools. This implied building capacity—not just holding educators accountable. Fourth, while many educational improvement services were offered and provided to low-performing schools and districts to build their capacity, increases in performance were sporadic and often fleeting for multiple reasons, not least of which was an inability to change the infrastructure that unintentionally perpetuated and reinforced poor-quality teaching. Faddism in educational programs, a revolving door of superintendents within specific districts, poor teacher recruiting and retention, and a lack of support from the community all contrived to ensure that progress was marginal in many locales.

It was in this environment that the Ford Foundation, frustrated with attempts at encouraging the improvement of educational services in our inner cities, began an initiative it hoped would bring about more sustained change. The foundation called its effort the Collaborating for Education Reform Initiative (CERI). In 1997, it funded several sites to build collaboratives among existing organizations in the hope of centering and sustaining educational improvement. In fall 1999, the Ford Foundation asked RAND to begin a formative evaluation of the effort.

This report describes RAND's findings concerning the progress made by those sites selected by the Ford Foundation and the lessons learned to date—i.e., four years into the effort to build collaboratives intended to sustain focused reform.

The remainder of this introduction provides the reader with the foundation's rationale for the CERI and the role RAND played. It then summarizes the research questions and methodology used. Finally, it outlines the rest of this report.

The Problem That Concerned the Ford Foundation

According to its mission statement (Ford Foundation, 2002),

> "The Ford Foundation is a resource for innovative people and institutions worldwide. [Its] goals are to:
> - Strengthen democratic values,
> - Reduce poverty and injustice,
> - Promote international cooperation, and
> - Advance human achievement."

In working toward reaching its goals, the Ford Foundation has been steadfastly interested in promoting a high-quality education for all students. It and others have been aware of the great disparity of educational outcomes among and between groups in the United States (Grissmer, 2000). As such, it has advanced a vision of educational reform. "The Ford Foundation supports education reform efforts that seek to improve the educational achievement of a large number of students and promote system-wide changes in policies and practices. Experience has demonstrated that school-by-school reforms may help some children achieve, but often prove difficult to scale-up and may not provide comparable educational opportunities for students as they continue on to higher grades" (Ford Foundation, 1999, p. 1).

Reform can have many meanings, but the intent of the Ford Foundation staff, evident from interviews and documents, was specifically *to improve the quality of teaching and learning in classrooms and schools in fundamental ways to improve student outcomes.*

Prior Reform Efforts

Efforts at reform of the public education system go back to the creation of the system itself and have evolved over time. In the past century, they have included the progressive reforms to create a more scientifically administered system in the 1920s and 1930s; civil rights efforts in the 1940s through 1960s leading to the Brown decision and all its repercussions; federal and state legislation in the 1960s and 1970s enacting compensatory education programs and later inclusion of special education and bilingual students under this umbrella; and the 1980s' moves toward decentralization, such as those in Chicago and Kentucky. In the 1990s, public schooling moved toward standards-based accountability. This movement culminated in the more recently passed No Child Left Behind Act.

With all this as a canvas, foundations, including the Ford Foundation, have more quietly tried in recent years to build capacity in local areas. The Ford Foundation's instincts about how to address failures to significantly improve the quality of teaching in urban districts was shaped by its knowledge of several strands of reform, as well as its own experiences in supporting collaborative formation to increase the college graduation rates of minority students. The following provides a brief description of the different local reform approaches and efforts that the foundation considered in developing CERI.

School Operations and Functions. One set of local reform approaches focuses directly on schools and attempts to direct changes in administrator and teacher behaviors, governance, curriculum and instruction, and student assignment. These are usually promulgated by the district or state or by external agents of the district, such as professional development consultants, design teams, etc. Recent examples include the Comprehensive School Reform Demonstration Program; Class Size Reduction in Tennessee or California; subject-specific program interventions, such as the adoption of Open Court Literacy, Balanced Literacy, and Everyday Math; or significant professional development of teachers to improve their practice.

Students and Families. Another set of local approaches focuses on individual students and their families—attempting to engage them more fully in the educational enterprise. These can be directed from the school but have also been developed and implemented by churches, universities, parent groups, and business partners. They emphasize such interventions as mentoring, volunteerism, career counseling, after-school programs, integrated social services, and parental involvement in overseeing homework, participating in the PTA, governance, and fundraising.

System-Level Improvement or Systemic Policy Reform. Another approach focuses on local support for public education—attempting either to encourage improvement through systemic reorganization or reallocation or to enable change through increased resources (bonds, tax base, financial equity). The former can be undertaken by the central office. The latter efforts usually are initiated and supported by forces outside of the school organization: concerned citizens, public education funds, private support for such groups as the Edison Project, or wider political interests.

Through internal discussions and examination of existing initiatives, the foundation staff became convinced that specific sites could make high-quality teaching in all classrooms a reality by utilizing a combination of the above approaches. These included such actions as effectively linking the different levels of pre-K through 12 and higher-education systems; promoting informed public dialogue, debate, and consensus-building around school reform options; promoting professional development for faculty, staff, and administrators; promoting district and state policy changes; and enhancing the role of parents and caregivers (Ford Foundation, 1999, p. 1).

The intention of all these actions was on changing the organization and culture of schools, their relationships with constituencies, and the systems in which they are embedded. Furthermore, the Ford sponsors believed that the more coherent, steady, and coordinated these multiple approaches were, the more likely they would be to succeed where other disjointed or discontinuous efforts had failed.

Strategy Chosen by the Ford Foundation

The Ford Foundation translated this belief into a strategy for reform: *collaboration*. This philosophy grew out of, in part, sharing lessons from other foundations' experiences with collaborative efforts including the Annenberg Challenge Grants and the Pew Charitable Trust's Systemic Initiative. It was also a result of the Ford Foundation's own previous efforts at collaboration supported from 1991 to 2000 called the Urban Partnership Program (UPP). The goal of UPP was "to increase the number of low income and minority students who successfully enter and complete college and embark upon careers so that by all measures of academic success, their rates of attainment equal those of more affluent, majority students." The program was "initiated as recognition grew that increasing the number of two-year and four-year college graduates in an urban community was a sufficiently complex task that required the attention of the whole community." Citywide teams in 16 communities were established to work collaboratively toward the goal. Successes of the UPP initiative had convinced Ford staff that collaboration among organizations and institutions within a community could be a powerful solution to the erratic and marginal nature of urban reform efforts.

Based on its own experiences with the UPP initiative and knowledge of other reform efforts, the Ford Foundation chose to encourage the formation of collaboratives composed of community-based organizations in urban settings to address systemic barriers to high-quality teaching and learning. By basing the impetus for reform largely outside of the public school central office, the foundation hoped to avoid the pattern of failure of reforms that originated in the central office and were led by a "transformational," often brief-tenured, superintendent. These internal efforts often dissipated when district leadership turned over. The Ford Foundation envisioned collaboratives with multiple member organizations that could outlive the administrations of public officials. Furthermore, it hoped that collaborative-supported reforms would also potentially avoid the failures associated with internally mandated reforms that are not supported by the community or by school personnel. By working from the outside inward and by involving school staff in planning and constructing the interventions, Ford sponsors hoped that buy-in and commitment to reform efforts would increase.

The foundation translated its ideas about how to improve and sustain systemic reform into the new CERI program, by issuing a series of planning grants in July 1997. As stated in the subsequent implementation request for proposals (RFP), "system-wide reform efforts require effective coalitions among organizations which are committed to systemic educational reform over an extended period of time and who project their efforts to the state-level" (Ford Foundation, 1999, p. 1). Note that the term used here was "coalition." The foundation itself did not have a strongly developed sense of who should be involved in collaboration or how, only that local institutions working together might be more effective than local institutions working against each other. We will discuss this issue of the lack of strong definition in Chapter Three.

Figure 1.1 provides an overview of the foundation's theory of change. The foundation would provide individual sites with funds, general goals, and some technical assistance to develop collaboratives. These sites would have to both develop collaboratives as well as carry out collaborative activities. Collaborative activities were to be directed at three possible groups within the community: the district and supporting educational infrastructures; a feeder pattern of schools referred to as a cluster and including teachers, parents, and students; and the larger community, including families and voters. In turn, these activities were expected to result in changes to classroom-level teaching and learning. This in turn would bring about improved stu-

Figure 1.1
General Conception of CERI

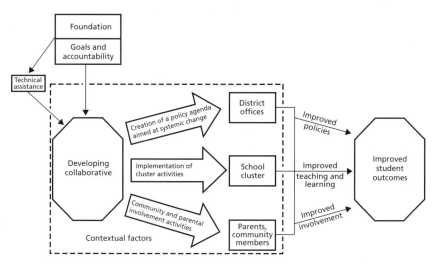

dent outcomes. Finally, contextual factors, indicated by the dotted box in the figure, would affect not only the building of the collaboratives and the issues chosen for activities but also the implementation of the activities.

Admittedly, this conception is very general. In the next chapter, we provide a more specific description of the foundation's evolving concept.

The foundation proposed a developmental initiative set in real-life communities. As part of this effort, it asked the developing collaboratives to work initially in a cluster of schools within a district—usually a feeder pattern of elementary and middle schools and a high school. The idea was to establish interventions at the smallest local level that could then be expanded throughout the district.

The Ford Foundation encouraged sites to develop unique interventions at the cluster level to improve the quality of teaching and learning but within three specific areas: more coherent professional development, improved K–12 alignment, and increased parental involvement.

The foundation stressed these three areas largely because staff members' experiences led them to believe that other reform efforts had been successful in these areas. For example, several partnerships sponsored by the foundation between schools of education and K–12 schools had been established across the country to address teacher professional development and K–16 alignment. Also, other efforts—often consisting of at least one community-based organization—had undertaken initiatives aimed at building parental involvement.

The Ford Foundation also encouraged broader initiatives to improve community engagement and to enact systemic policy changes that would sustain reforms. The rationale for working in these areas was grounded in the foundation's theory that community-based collaboratives could build and maintain commitment to reform efforts by generating buy-in and by pressuring districts to implement and sustain systemic changes. The foundation tended to emphasize these two areas increasingly over time.

Each site was awarded $300,000 per year, but we note here that the funds provided were not enough, and were not meant to be enough, to fund a districtwide reform effort. The Ford Foundation never meant to provide the financial wherewithal for that level of effort. Rather, given the existence of community-based organizations in each setting that were interested in education improvement and the existing efforts by schools and their district, the funds were to be used to develop collaboratives to unite the community-based organizations, schools, and their respective districts in ways that could produce greater levels of improvement and a stronger, more consistent focus on the reform agenda. The foundation meant for the grants to act as a multiplier for existing efforts—glue, as it were, to cement the reform efforts over the long haul. As such, a major expected outcome was strong interorganizational linkages among the groups and institutions within the community, enabling stronger implementation of the school improvement effort in the cluster and eventually in the community. Later we will define organizational linkages more carefully, but it is enough here to indicate that the foundation was striving for a jointly held vision and set of actions among groups that were complementary and mutually reinforcing rather than in conflict.

Description of CERI Sites

To begin CERI, the foundation extended implementation grants to organizations in eight communities in 1998 and 1999. Table 1.1 shows the sites, the name of each collaborative, the lead organization, the number of partners, and the number of schools in the cluster as indicated in each site's original implementation grant applications.

Table 1.1
CERI Sites in the First Year

Site	Name	Lead Organization	Number of Partners	Cluster: Number of Schools
Cataño, P.R.	San Juan Metro Alliance for Education	Sacred Heart University	5	Cataño school district: 11 schools
Charlotte-Mecklenburg, N.C.	Collaboration for Education Reform	Charlotte-Mecklenburg Schools	7	West Mecklenburg feeder area: 10 schools
Denver, Colo.	Denver Collaborative for Educational Reform	Public Education and Business Coalition	9	Eastside and Westside feeder areas: 9 schools
D.C.	DC VOICE	Network for Educators in the Americas	19	Columbia Heights/Shaw feeder areas: 6 schools
Jackson, Miss.	Ask For More	Parents for Public Schools	6	Lanier feeder area: 12 schools
Miami–Dade County, Fla.	Central Express	Greater Miami Urban Education Pact	8	Central feeder area: 11 schools
San Antonio, Tex.	ACCESS	Intercultural Development Research Association	6	Burbank feeder area: 9 schools
Santa Ana, Calif.	Above the Mean	Santa Ana Public School District	9	Area II feeder area: 12 schools plus district teen-parent program

Purpose and Audience of the Report

In fall 1999, RAND undertook a formative evaluation of the effort as requested by the Ford Foundation. The evaluation had three purposes: to provide feedback to sites to improve their efforts, to provide information to the foundation to inform its decisions about support and funding provided to sites; and to document for the public the progress made under this collaborative initiative. The research questions were:

- Did sites show progress toward desired outcomes? If not, why not? If so, why? What other effects occurred?
- Could lessons or promising practices be discerned from the experiences of individual collaboratives or the group as a whole?
- Could collaboratives be effectively created by an outside influence, such as the Ford Foundation, to sustain education improvement efforts?

Methodology

CERI is a development effort suitable for study using an embedded case study approach with each collaborative and its surrounding community as a single embedded case. As described in more detail in the next chapter, we used mixed methods. We collected and analyzed extensive field interviews, documents, survey data, and quantitative data supplied by districts and schools to assess the individual and comparative progress of sites.

Remainder of the Report

In Chapter Two, we provide a conceptual framework based in the literature and the indicators of progress and methodology used to assess site evolution. In Chapter Three, we provide a general history of the initiative and a synopsis of initial conditions at the sites to orient the reader to the challenges faced by the collaboratives. Chapter Four answers the first research question by providing a synopsis of progress made across the sites organized around the indictors. It describes our assessment of sites' progress as of spring 2003. Chapter Five answers the second research question by providing themes that we take from this experience, tentative though they are. The final chapter provides conclusions and recommendations. It is followed by an appendix that contains more detailed information on each site.

CHAPTER TWO

Literature Review, Indicators, and Methodology

In this chapter we review the literature to develop a set of indicators useful for judging progress among the sites. We then describe our methodology for measuring the indicators in each of the eight sites.

Literature Review

Two literatures seemed relevant to the Ford Foundation's policy hypothesis: the literature on collaboratives interested in improving social or education services and the literature on implementation of education reforms. We reviewed these with three main goals: to help define terms, to help develop useful expectations for progress, and to help define specific indicators of more-general concepts when possible.

Levels of Interorganizational Linkages

The literature on interorganizational collaboration to support social and educational reforms consists largely of case studies of existing or attempted collaboration. The case studies typically included qualitative descriptions of such collaborative efforts as school-community partnerships, teacher collaboratives, and partnerships between neighborhood and community-based organizations, to name a few. Often absent are generically expressed expectations for progress or outcomes. None of the studies is statistical or includes controls or strong comparison groups. While the literature does not provide strong empirical evidence of outcomes produced by collaborative efforts, it has produced some useful definitions and typologies. Definitions were important to our work given that the foundation did not define what it meant by collaboration.

The following paragraphs mesh several frameworks separately developed by Hogue (1994), Keith (1993), Mattessich and Monsey (1992), Himmelman (1996), Lieberman and McLaughlin (1992), and Winer and Ray (1997) into one useful for the purposes of this report.

Our review of the literature on interorganizational linkages to improve social welfare indicates several different levels of possible interactions among organizations. Networking is the lowest and most informal level. Cooperation and or coordination require higher levels of interorganizational linkages. Some authors refer to these alternatively as partnerships and coalitions. Finally, collaboration represents the greatest level of interorganizational linking. While disagreeing on the names of levels in between networking and collaboration, all authors agree that "collaboration" is the most complete and integrated level of inter-organizational linkage.

Networking. Himmelman (1996), Hogue (1994), Keith (1993), and Lieberman and McLaughlin (1992) all define networking in common terms emphasizing the exchange of information for mutual benefit. Networking can increase dialogue among members of organizations, create a common understanding of problems and possible solutions, provide a clearinghouse for information, and create a base of support for new ideas. It often reflects an initial level of trust, limited time availability, and a reluctance to share turf. Network structures, compared to more fully developed linkages, tend to be flexible with roles of participants loosely defined.

Cooperation and Coordination. While such authors as Melaville and Blank (1991), Mattessich and Monsey (1992), Himmelman (1996), and Winer and Ray (1997) differ in how they name the next level—cooperation or coordination—in general, all agree that someplace between networking and full collaboration lies a set of inter-organizational linkages that expand past networking to include jointly held goals and some cooperative activities. The focus is on short-term informal relations that exist without any clearly defined mission, structure, or planning effort for the group of organizations as a whole. Each organization maintains its individual mission, goals, and programs. Cooperative partners share information only about the subject at hand. Each organization retains authority and keeps resources separate.

Collaboration. The strongest form of interorganizational linkage is collaboration. Melaville and Blank (1991, p. 14) describe collaboration as partnerships that establish common goals.

"In order to address problems that lie beyond any single agency's exclusive purview, but which concern them all, partners agree to pool resources, jointly plan, implement, and evaluate new services and procedures, and delegate individual responsibility for the outcomes of their joint efforts." Wenger (1998) suggests that a "joint enterprise" is kept together by "joint work." A definition of joint work provided by Marsh (2002, p. 8) is that it "results from a collective process of negotiation, is defined and owned by participants, and creates a sense of mutual accountability." At the system level, "collaborative ventures are empowered—politically, by virtue of their members' collective 'clout,' or legally, by the state or other entity—to negotiate, as well as to advocate for, programs and policies leading to more comprehensive service delivery." Collaborations bring previously separate organizations into a new structure with full commitment to a common mission. Collaborative strategies are appropriate in localities where the need and intent is to change fundamentally the way services are designed and delivered (Melaville and Blank, 1991, p. 14).

Several studies taken together imply the following manifestations of a well-functioning collaborative (School Communities That Work, 2002; Keith, 1993; Kaganoff, 1998; Stone, 1998; Tushnet, 1993; Mattessich and Monsey, 1992; Dluhy, 1990).[1]

- Consensus governance with equal representation of each organization and shared responsibility

---

[1] We note that the authors cited do not always define what is meant by "well-functioning" or what outcomes are associated with these factors.

- Strong, legitimizing leadership that builds commitment to common goals
- Open and clear communication among partners
- A strong sense of the community and its particular problems, leading to clearly identified goals with agreed to, specific results to pursue
- Engagement in evaluation, adaptive planning, and assessment of progress from a strong baseline of data
- Engagement in building civic capacity, defined as "the mobilization of stakeholders in support of a community-wide cause" (Stone, 1998, p. 15)
- Pooled resources
- A long-term commitment or a view toward sustainment of the work, including plans to build funding streams to support it.

Note that none of the studies we found examined concrete outcomes or goals in terms of specific changes in the local communities. Neither did they associate these goals systematically with the activities of the collaboratives. Thus, the noted benefits are largely organizational in nature and say little about whether collaboratives with these characteristics have a higher probability than others of actually producing reforms. The literature points to several benefits of collaborative approaches: efficiency in provision of resources; individual efficacy for members; and integration of expertise and resources. Keith (1993) also described contextual factors that contribute to strong collaborative formation.

- The community has a history of working together cooperatively (Mattessich and Monsey [1992] also point this out)
- Existing strong and widespread support for educational reform
- Supportive policies, laws, and regulations
- Availability of necessary resources—contextual, in-kind, financial, and human
- A recognized problem or reason for the collaboration to exist that requires a comprehensive response

- A convener that calls an initial meeting to draw possible partners into a dialog about possible solutions to a situation.

Several authors (Keith, 1993; Kaganoff, 1998; Himmelman, 1996; Iwanowsky, 1996; and Baker, 1993) point to the challenges involved in setting up effective collaboratives, including the need to make sufficient time for relationships to develop, the difficulty of balancing risk and benefits among partners, the difficulty of building and reinforcing structural and institutional supports, and a failure to agree on basic goals and approaches.

Expectations for Implementation

The foundation's goal of improving teaching and learning in classrooms requires significant changes in behaviors of students, teachers, principals, and administrators if the other goal of improved student outcomes was to be met. Attempting to fundamentally change the behaviors and tasks of staff in organizations is one of the most difficult reforms to accomplish. This is especially true when multiple levels of government are involved; when significantly different behaviors are called for; when the tasks and behaviors are those of a large and diverse group; and when these actors have varying incentives to change (Mazmanian and Sabatier, 1989). In schools, these groups respond to and are driven by many varying incentives, rules, and regulations inherent in the infrastructure of schools and schooling (Gitlin and Margonis, 1995; Cuban, 1984; Huberman and Miles, 1984).

Many previous studies of implementation of school reform have highlighted that local capacity and will are ultimately the two factors that determine successful implementation:

> Policy makers can't mandate what matters most: local capacity and will . . . environmental stability, competing centers of authority, contending priorities or pressures and other aspects of the social-political milieu can influence implementer willingness profoundly. . . . Change is ultimately a problem of the smallest unit. (McLaughlin, 1987, pp. 172–173.)

The foundation recognized this but hoped that collaboration among the different local agencies and community-based organizations would bring about coherence instead of the more normal competition and fragmentation. A characteristic of success, therefore, was whether the collaborative could encourage changes in policies to make them more supportive of improved teaching and learning. Another was whether the collaborative gained stature in the community such that it either brought these different groups together to work toward supportive policy or participated in governing structures that made more coherent policy.

What is often true, however, is that attempts at implementation of specific interventions aimed at teaching lead to "mutual adaptation" with local educational agencies, school staff, and intermediaries changing behaviors in significant, but nonuniform and unexpected, ways (Berman et al., 1975). As McLaughlin put it, "Local variability is the rule; uniformity is the exception" (1991, p. 13). The original users of the term "mutual adaptation" meant to invoke a benign or positive process of movement toward mutually agreed-on goals with the intervention changing for the better in some sense so as to support those goals.

Two other factors are important in understanding what could be expected from the sites in terms of full implementation. The first is that the foundation did not prescribe a set of interventions—sets of interventions were being developed by the collaboratives as they worked. Second, the collaboratives each had different starting places and contexts—and therefore different appropriate interventions as well as starting points in terms of local will and capacity. Given these differences, we should expect significant variation among the sites in terms of both starting points and progress.

Others have found that adaptation does not always lead to enhancement of the original policy or necessarily promote the desired performance outcomes. These less-benign effects have been categorized in different ways as unanticipated consequences, including disappearance, erosion, dilution, drift, or simply slowed implementation (Cuban, 1984; Pressman and Wildavsky, 1973; Daft, 1995; Mazmanian and Sabatier, 1989; Weatherley and Lipsky, 1977; Yin, 1979).

These could be expected as well, especially if collaboratives failed in their efforts to foster will and the community did not have the capacity to support the desired changes.

It is often the case that these less-desirable outcomes occur because policymakers do not put in place needed support mechanisms or do not change the supporting infrastructure to help the external agent implement the intervention. McDonnell and Grubb (1991) make clear that successful implementation of any educational mandate, whether by an external agent or by the school itself, requires support of the implementers, capacity on their part to follow through on the mandate, and some enforcement or incentives to support compliance. The building of capacity requires the infusion of resources in terms of time, funding, and information—social and intellectual. These resources are often referred to as "slack" or "slack resources," without which reform cannot be successfully undertaken. Capacity cannot be mandated but must be built with slack resources.

The education literature points to important supports that can lead to implementation closer to that desired. These conditions include the following (McLaughlin, 1991):

- active participation and support of district leadership, including the removal of conflicting priorities and initiatives;
- funding to get the initiative under way and to indicate its importance;
- understanding by stakeholders and implementers of the intervention and its intended effects gained through clear communication;
- specific attention and assistance for implementation, such as:
  — concrete and specific teacher training including classroom assistance by local staff;
  — teacher observations of similar projects in like settings;
  — stakeholder acceptance of the initiative and participation in project decisions, as well as regular project meetings focused on practical issues; and
  — local development of project material.

This set of findings brings us back to the foundation's urging of collaboratives to not just encourage implementation of specific interventions, such as a professional development module around math or literacy instruction, but also to encourage the development and implementation of supporting policies, such as monitoring, provision of incentives, and follow-up coaching that ensures that teachers effectively use the module to deliver their pedagogy and curriculum. Thus, it emphasized policy efforts and political actions to bring actors together and to develop more coherence.

This literature provides a rationale for the foundation's theory of action and provides some criteria (albeit somewhat vague) that can assess progress toward a more coherent or systemic reform agenda. "Systemic" is used here to indicate the need for supporting and mutually reinforcing policies, political leadership, and communication strategies, meshed with specific interventions aimed at high-quality teaching and learning.

Implementation is a progressive activity, with full implementation sometimes only evident after several stages of activity (Mazmanian and Sabatier, 1989; Yin, 1979). This phenomenon occurs in part because of the developmental nature of some interventions, but it can also stem from the cycles of political support and interest that come and go depending on the values of leaders in office, competing policy issues, and the funding picture.

Implications

The above has several implications for expectations concerning the progress of the Ford Foundation–funded collaboratives:

- Collaborative efforts are a challenge in and of themselves and one should expect them to develop slowly and perhaps unevenly. Results both in terms of gaining a functioning collaborative and the effectiveness of that collaborative in enabling positive educational improvements might take several years and might not run smoothly. Many examples exist of collaboratives that have failed to grow and develop, implying that the success of this approach is not certain.

- Partners might go through different levels of interorganizational linkages, including networks, cooperation and coordination, and finally collaboration. Progress might be driven by many different factors, but two in particular: whether the leadership promotes or inhibits collaborative functions, and whether relevant stakeholders are involved in the collaborative.

- Collaboration as the mechanism to encourage change poses implementation issues in that it requires new behaviors and coordination among the members of the collaborative. This is in addition to the new behaviors desired for teachers, school personnel, parents, and district managers. In short, two levels of changed behaviors are needed with many actors involved.

- Contexts in the sites are expected to have strong impacts on whether the collaboratives successfully form and function. In particular, strong past collaborative histories, existing community understanding and agreement about the problem and need for comprehensive solutions, and adequate resources—including human—are likely to be associated with progress.

- Finally, actual implementation of the collaborative strategies and plans should be expected to vary for several reasons, not just collaborative function. The more supportive the collaborative can be in terms of encouraging participation of leadership, enabling funding for reform, clearly communicating with stakeholders, and providing specific assistance, then the more likely the implementation will be to progress as the collaborative desires.

Characteristics or Indicators of Progress

Rather than a simple theory of change, this literature points to a very complex process that, because of the multiple factors and actors involved, might or might not lead to improved classroom practices and reinforcing support policies that encourage improved student outcomes. At the core of this report are five dimensions, grounded in research on collaboratives, across which we assess site progress:

- The level of development of interorganizational linkages
- The level of development and implementation of plans for improving quality teaching and learning in the cluster
- The level of development and implementation of plans for systemic changes in policy
- The level of independence achieved by the collaborative
- The level of change in student outcomes as a result of collaborative actions.

Interorganizational Linkages

The level of development of the interorganizational linkages could be assessed as corresponding to the three levels indicated in the literature. Sites operating at the lowest level, *networking*, would show only evidence of information-sharing among partners, with perhaps some nascent forays into coordinated actions. Sites operating at the next-highest levels, *cooperative partnerships*, would show evidence of shared or common goals and visions and successfully coordinated actions. Sites operating at the highest level, *collaboration*, would indicate that the partners were collectively involved in greater levels of joint activities, as manifested by a collective process of negotiation, with activities defined and jointly owned by participants, and a sense of mutual accountability.

- Information-sharing—Sharing of information among members both to form cohesion of purpose and to coordinate actions.
- Shared goals—Strong buy-in to the goals of the collaborative by all members.
- Routine collection and sharing of data for problem identification—Members jointly collect and review data on a regular basis.
- Effective joint decisionmaking—Decisionmaking structures and leadership that encourages joint decisionmaking and joint actions. Here, we would distinguish between top-down decisionmaking and more authentic collaborative interactions, regardless of the formal governance structure.

- Resource pooling—Organizations combine resources (foundation funding, personnel time, and other sources of funding) to pursue the collaborative mission, as opposed to funneling foundation grants to the members for existing operations.
- Joint actions—Organizations develop activities together and implement them jointly, as opposed to implementing the existing activities of each partner in parallel or with some level of coordination, and hold each other accountable for the outcomes.
- Shared products—Joint actions lead to joint products of the members—clearly labeled as from the group, not the individual members.
- Member rationale is clear, with important constituencies included—The composition of partnerships is logical to all involved and includes all relevant stakeholders.
- Active involvement of the school staff and parents—The literature indicates that the involvement of stakeholders is key to implementation. The foundation encouraged active involvement of school staff and parents in the collaboratives as part of the strategy to improve quality teaching and learning in a specific cluster of schools.
- Stability of members over time—Stability of the collaborative structure would not be seen as a sign of a well-functioning collaborative in and of itself. Given the quick start-up, we would expect several of the grantees, especially the ones without a previous history of collaboration, to experience some instability as they attempted to develop a vision and find a purpose in the larger context of education improvement in their locale. Instability, however, with constant reorganizations, would be viewed as a sign that the collaborative had not taken hold as expected.

Among our sites, some partners might accomplish information-sharing and little else. These would be labeled as at the level of networking. Those sites whose partners worked to coordinate some of the above activities would be considered coordinating partners. Those who accomplished this full set of activities and did so in a manner indicative of true jointness, not merely coordination, would be labeled collaboratives.

The Level of Development and Implementation of Plans for Achieving High-Quality Teaching and Learning in the Cluster

Given that each site was encouraged to develop different interventions in the cluster to improve teaching and learning, we developed a scheme for judging progress that was not dependent on the specific activities involved. The scheme had to recognize that the foundation's intention was for activities developed within each cluster to eventually be adopted across their respective districts. The implementation literature provides a simple spectrum for assessing progress no matter what the particular goals of the activities (Bodilly et al., 1998). Progress can be seen for any specific activity as being at one of four levels, which have been slightly adopted for CERI's purposes:

- *Planning*—Majority of activities are in the planning stage with members busy discussing and developing ideas. Recall each site was given a planning year. Thus, our expectations were that every site would at least be at this level. If a site constantly changed the activities, we labeled it as being still at the planning stage.
- *Piloting or demonstrating*—Majority of activities have moved toward implementation with a selected or small number of cluster schools, teachers, parents, or students.
- *Implementing*—Majority of activities have moved toward implementation across most of the targeted subjects within the cluster.
- *Expanding*—Activities have been adopted by the district or by a significant number of schools outside the cluster or district.

Because the sites had many different activities proposed at any one time, we tried to assess whether the majority was at one of these levels. In reality, often times different activities were at different levels within a site. Thus, some subjective leveling is involved.

The Level of Development and Implementation of Plans for Systemic Changes in Policy

The foundation expected the efforts of sites to lead to systemwide changes in policy. For example, if a site worked with a cluster to align curriculum across grade levels, the foundation expected sites to encourage districtwide curriculum alignment. We adopted the same spectrum as above to assess the progress made with respect to systemic policy interventions:

- *Planning*—Majority of policy activities are in the planning stage with members busy discussing and developing ideas.
- *Piloting or demonstrating*—Majority of activities have moved toward implementation within a selected number of schools, teachers, parents, or students, etc. For example, the collaborative might have identified teacher retention as a serious problem within the district and proposed a set of changes to existing recruiting and teacher mentoring policies. The district might agree to pilot the ideas in one or two schools and, if successful, change the policy across the district.
- *Implementing*—The majority of activities have moved toward implementation across most of the targeted subjects within the district. Using the example above, the district would agree to change the policies regarding teacher retention and institute new policy across the district.
- *Expanding*—The activities have been adopted by other districts or have affected state policy.

The Level of Independence Achieved by the Collaborative

The foundation expected the sites to eventually become independent of the need for foundation funds. In part, this is a common expectation of foundations that do not wish to be seen as permanently attached to a site. Independence can also be seen as a sign that the collaborative has become successful. It might imply that the collaborative has grown to the point that it is fully functioning as a private nonprofit, that it is able to charge fees for its work, or that other groups or funders find the activities so compelling that they provide further support.

While three to four years might be too soon to expect complete independence, it is unlikely that this would happen unless the collaboratives had at least made plans to move in this direction. We assessed the progress made toward independence using levels similar to the above:

- *Planning*—Majority of sustainment activities are in the planning stage with members busy discussing and developing ideas.
- *Significant Moves Toward Independence*—Through whatever means the site has developed significant funding sources apart from the Ford Foundation to carry out the functions of CERI.
- *Fully Independent*—The level of funding sources has enabled the site to become completely independent while still maintaining the CERI activities.

The Level of Change in Student Outcomes as a Result of Collaborative Actions

The foundation and the sites agreed that the purpose of the collaborative was to improve student outcomes. Therefore, we tracked student outcomes for all the sites over time. We attempted—where possible—to gain access to student-level data to understand the full impact of collaboratives' work, accounting for students who stayed in their respective cluster versus those who moved in and out of them. The following are the indicators of improved outcomes we attempted to track across sites:

- Test score gains
- Improved course taking, especially increased percentages of students taking gate-keeper courses
- Improved attendance
- Reduced mobility
- Increased percentage of students making the transition to English proficiency
- Increasing high school completion rates

- Improved traditional indicators of teacher quality, such as fewer emergency credentialed teachers and less teacher turnover
- Improved postsecondary outcomes.

It is difficult to attribute changes in final student outcomes to the activities of the grantees for several reasons:

- Data limitations made it difficult to make strong connections between interventions and outcomes. While we tracked test scores and other data in most sites, individual student-level data were usually not available. In several cases, the test instruments changed during the initiative, making comparisons across years difficult. Additionally, the collaborative did not always track which teachers had received training.
- CERI interventions took place at the same time as other reform efforts and their effects could not be disentangled.
- In several sites, the interventions did not have face value in terms of connections to student outcomes.
- In several cases, the interventions were implemented inconsistently and or poorly, making any impact questionable.

Data limitation issues were discussed with the foundation early in the project. A decision was made to proceed with this data collection and analysis to help sites see what could be done with the data at hand and to help everyone understand the contrasts among sites. As we discuss later, this data collection and analysis—the results of which we provided annually to the foundation and sites—proved useful in initiating discussions about how to use data.

In the following chapters, we do not stress the outcome measures and their relation to the work of the collaboratives. First, as mentioned, the data itself were of poor quality. Second, several sites did not make enough progress to have the effects they desired. Finally, given the slow development of some collaboratives, it might be too soon to expect strong shifts in student outcomes. We note, therefore, if a prima facie case could be made that the site developed and implemented an intervention to a level where an impact could be expected. If this was the case, then we provide a brief discussion of whether data provided evidence that an impact might have occurred (i.e., test scores shifted in the expected direction). In no case could we prove that the collaborative was responsible for the changes observed.

Methodology

CERI is a development effort suitable for study using qualitative approaches including descriptive analysis and supported by quantitative analysis. In our effort to assess collaborative formation and the progress made toward desired outcomes, we chose an embedded case study approach as most appropriate for the study. Each collaborative and its surrounding community were viewed as a single embedded case. In attempting to understand the progress made, the unit of analysis was the collaborative and its impact on the educational improvement effort within its community. We first attempted to understand whether and how a collaborative developed and functioned within the community. Then, we attempted to assess progress of the collaborative toward its stated goals and the effect of the collaboratives' work within the surrounding community. Finally, we looked for evidence of institutionalization of the collaboratives' work and sustainment of activities. We also looked for evidence of systematic changes across the district.

Ideally, an evaluation should distinguish between outcomes associated with other activities in the sites and outcomes associated with the grantees' activities. Districts and states might already have a community involvement initiative under way that eventually results in improvement for some students. This change in student performance could not be attributed to the grant. It is also important to understand the "value added" of the Ford grant to the existing system and not to assume that the initiative produced all the outcomes (be they positive or negative) of the current reform agenda at the sites.

We did not think, given the nature of the initiative described above, that it would be possible to distinguish these effects. Practically then, it was more prudent to ask if the collaboratives' efforts at each site helped in any way. Given the developmental and context-constrained nature of the collaboratives, it was highly unlikely that comparisons to other districts would provide useful information. The following comparisons, however, could provide some insights about progress and impact:

- Comparison of sites to themselves before, during, and after the initiative to understand degrees of improvement.
- Comparisons to each other to arrive at overall lessons or promising practices.
- Comparisons of changes in student performance characteristics to district and state averages over time to understand if they equaled or exceeded those averages.

Data Sources

We used mixed methods in the analysis, collecting both qualitative and quantitative data to make the analytic comparisons described above.

Document Review. We tracked major newspapers in each area to understand the different educational issues and initiatives under way and collected plans, brochures, flyers, and other materials created and distributed by each collaborative.

Yearly Site Visits with Fieldwork. RAND researchers spent four to five days at each site each year. During that time, we met individually with members of the collaborative to understand the extent of each collaborative's activities and how the Ford Foundation grant monies were being used.

We also visited four schools in each cluster, usually two elementary schools, one middle school, and one high school. In each school, we interviewed the principal for approximately one hour about school climate, recent changes in the school, professional development, and community support. We interviewed teachers in groups of four to five. We met individual teachers or department heads in such key subject areas as math and science, especially when these were the focus of the collaborative. We interviewed school counselors and any other school personnel assisting with collaborative efforts. When warranted, we met with staff involved in extra-school programs, such as tutoring, after-school programs, and family centers. In some of the sites we also got permission to meet with students.

At the district level, RAND staff interviewed selected school board members, the superintendent of schools, the director of testing and evaluation, and the district contact for the collaborative. Interviews with supervisors for professional development, feeder pattern planning (usually the Assistant Superintendent for Curriculum and Instruction), and the budget were also conducted. Some school districts had key district personnel working to address critical issues specific to the area or state, such as class size in California, assessment in Texas, or bilingual education in Texas and California, and these were contacted as well.

Within the larger community, we interviewed or met with parent groups, contacts from churches, members of business partnerships, key politicians, and others who supported school reform and collaborative efforts. In some cases, the collaboratives had their own evaluators in place. We actively sought to discuss issues with these evaluators and understand their local evaluation efforts.

To the extent possible, we attempted to track progress of the unique initiatives specified by the sites. Site visits were coordinated with important collaborative and school activities, such as PTA, school board, or town meetings so that community members targeted by the collaborative could be interviewed and activities observed.

Teacher Surveys. In the first year of the study, we surveyed teachers in all the cluster schools at each of the eight sites. We gathered information on teacher background, teacher views of current professional development, teacher motivation, teacher efficacy, teacher participation in collaborative-sponsored interventions, and the level of support teachers received from the community. In year three, teachers were again surveyed, but only at five sites where it was deemed that the collaborative might have had an impact on teaching. In the other three sites, collaborative work concentrated in areas that the teacher survey did not tap.

Principal Phone Survey. In the second year of the study, we conducted phone interviews with each principal in the cluster schools associated with CERI. We asked questions about the schools' relationship with the collaborative, support they received from it, and about the district in terms of reform and progress being made toward goals.

UPP Phone Survey. In the third year of the study, we also conducted phone interviews with selected members of all the former UPP sites to understand whether partnerships were still in existence, what lessons had been learned about scale-up and sustainment of reform efforts, and what thoughts they had with regard to the usefulness of collaboration in promoting community reforms. While the principal and UPP phone surveys informed the findings included in this report, we do not directly present the results of these two surveys, but they were helpful in constructing realistic indicators and expectations.

Administrative and Outcome Data. With the help of key contacts in each school district, we gathered quantitative and qualitative data on student characteristics, performance indicators, community profiles, financial issues, available funding streams, and sites' systemic reform experience for the two years prior to the study and for the study years as well. In addition, we consistently gathered data specific to the collaborative and the community in general when they were available.

We do not use much of this information in this report, focusing on other collaborative formation, implementation, sustainment, and scale-up factors. Nevertheless, we provide this detail to help the reader learn what was collected and to be able to make several points later in the report about data use by the sites and RAND's role.

Table 2.1 details the type of data we were able to collect from each site. Publicly accessible outcome data were of particularly poor quality in Cataño, D.C., and Jackson. In Puerto Rico, we learned that the Commonwealth collects primarily handwritten data about schools and student performance each year, but these data are not systematically compiled and public access is not permitted. Data collection efforts by the central office in Jackson are comparatively weak because few resources are allocated to those tasks. In turn, the Missis-

Table 2.1
Data Availability for CERI Sites

	Level of Standardized Test Results	Other Student Outcomes					Teacher Quality	Post-Secondary Outcomes
		Course-Taking Patterns	Attendance	Mobility	English Proficiency	High School Completion Rates		
Cataño	Individual students[a]		X	X	N/A	Three years	X	
Charlotte	Individual students	X	X	X	X	One year	X	
Denver	Individual students[a]		X	X	X	One year		
District of Columbia	School averages[a]		X		X	Three years		
Jackson	School averages[a]	X	X			Three years		X
Miami	Individual students[a]	X	X	X	X	Three years	X	
San Antonio	Individual students	X	X	X	X	Four years	X	
Santa Ana	School averages	X	X		X	Four years	X	X

NOTE: Quantitative data were collected for two baseline school years, 1997–1998 and 1998–1999, and then during the years that CERI efforts were in full force, 1999–2000, 2000–2001, and 2001–2002. Data for the 2002–2003 school year did not become fully available until 2004.

[a] Tests administered were not consistent over the four academic years covered in this report.

X = Data were available, but was not necessarily consistent over four years.

sippi Department of Education does not provide test score and other information on its Web site in a format that is consistent over time. The D.C. central office does not maintain a Web site with current student performance data. Written reports are available on request, but again the data are not published in formats that allow for measurement of changes over time.

In contrast, central offices in Miami, Charlotte, San Antonio, Denver, and Santa Ana and their respective state departments of education offered a wide range of publicly accessible data that allowed for more in-depth analysis of changes in student performance and other interim outcomes over the past several years. Included were confidential individual student test scores and other student-specific characteristics that allowed for a tracking of individual students and more precise measurements of their academic achievements.

In spite of the differences in data quality, RAND reports of quantitative data in each site included a few measurements of student outcomes common across all sites. For example, all of the initial site proposals to the Ford Foundation stated intentions to decrease high school dropout rates, though none of the sites provided data measuring these rates over time. Because dropout rates published by state and central offices were not calculated with consistent measures and would not be comparable between sites, we used total enrollments in each grade level and the number of graduates to compile high school completion rates, which were comparable across all CERI sites. To calculate high school completion rates, we looked at cohorts of students and compared the number of students enrolled in ninth grade (or tenth grade for three-year high schools) one year to the number who graduated four (or three) years later. These rates are not precise, but in the absence of data on individual students, they provided a consistent measure that showed relative improvement over time. Students might leave a particular school between ninth grade and graduation for many reasons. Some may move out of the neighborhood or out of the district. Some may opt to attend private or magnet schools. Some may choose to earn high school credentials by taking the General Educational Development (GED) exam. Some may drop out. We expect, however, that as reforms become successful, school climate, teaching quality, and learning would improve and more students would choose to stay in school and at that particular school.

Another common measure across several sites consisted of tracking enrollments in college-prep courses. If reform efforts were successful, we would expect not only that more students stay in school but also that they choose to take courses at more advanced levels as well as more courses that are basic to preparation for college. In our analysis, we chose to focus on enrollment in high school math courses because math sequences are the most easily identified and most consistent across all sites. Other subjects are also required for college entrance, but they vary more from school to school in the types of courses offered.

In general, any student who plans to go to college needs at least one year of math beyond Algebra I. Specific course sequences vary in different districts or states. Sometimes students take a full-year of Algebra I, then a full-year of Algebra II. In some cases students take a year of geometry before the second year of algebra. We took these differences into account by combining all courses considered beginning algebra and pooling all courses beyond beginning algebra, labeling the latter advanced math.

Formative Feedback

During the course of this study, we provided annual case study reports to each site that utilized both quantitative and qualitative information, briefings to the sites at convenings, and formative feedback to the foundation.

Our formative feedback to the sites indicated the progress the sites had made along the five dimensions listed earlier. Organizing the reports in this way allowed us to frame our feedback to sites similarly. We reported the degree to which each site developed a collaborative structure, whether that structure had created and implemented plans consistent with improving teaching and learning, whether the collaborative had moved toward more systemic reform, whether it had made steps toward independence, and whether any outcomes were apparent.

CHAPTER THREE

History of CERI Reform

This chapter provides a synopsis of the overall CERI effort to orient the reader to the chronology of the unfolding initiative and the players involved. It also focuses on the evolving relationship between the key players, the foundation and the sites, and the increasing specificity of the initiative overtime. This chapter is crucial to understanding in broad terms the development of the entire effort. (The following chapter concentrates more on evolution of individual sites in lieu of this larger context.) This chapter first covers the request for proposals. Then it compares the sites and their characteristics early in the initiative. Finally, it provides a brief history of the remainder of the initiative up to summer 2003.

Request for Proposals

The Ford Foundation employed a two-step process to initiate CERI as shown in Figure 3.1. First, in 1997, about 12 UPP sites were given planning grants of up to $100,000 for one year to develop proposals that would state how the collaborative would proceed. In August 1998, the foundation selected three sites to receive implementation grants: Cataño, P.R.; Miami, Fla.; and Santa Ana, Calif. In 1998, 12 planning grants were again awarded to other sites familiar to the foundation, including several UPP sites that had not made the first round of cuts. In August 1999, the Ford Foundation selected an additional five communities (see Table 3.1) to be given implementation grants: Charlotte, N.C.; Denver, Colo.; Washington, D.C.; Jackson, Miss.; and San Antonio, Tex. In total, eight sites were chosen to receive annual implementation grants of $300,000 per year for two years ($600,000 total).

Figure 3.1
Timeline for the Effort

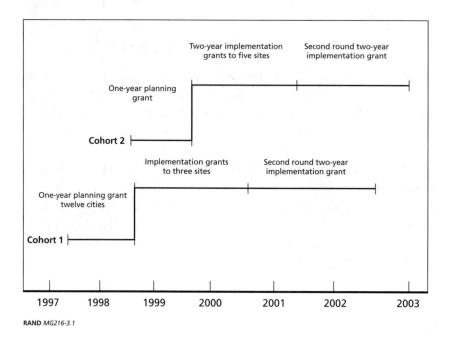

RAND MG216-3.1

Table 3.1
CERI Sites by Cohort

Cohort 1 Implementation Grant Awarded: August 1998	Cohort 2 Implementation Grant Awarded: August 1999
Cataño, P.R. Miami, Fla. Santa Ana, Calif.	Charlotte, N.C. Denver, Colo. Washington, D.C. Jackson, Miss. San Antonio, Tex.

In both iterations, all targeted organizations were asked to submit proposals in collaboration with other organizations in their respective communities to encourage and sustain K–12 reform efforts. The Ford Foundation specified the following essential elements:

- Collaborative efforts must promote systemwide education reform with the purpose of affecting a large number of students.
- Collaborative efforts must address the professional development of faculty, staff, administrators, and other leaders within the collaborative.
- Collaborative efforts must focus their reform efforts across at least three different levels of pre-K through 12 and higher-education systems within a feeder pattern or cluster of schools (i.e., elementary schools, middle schools, high schools, colleges).
- Collaborative efforts must plan to mobilize broad support for educational reform.
- Collaborative efforts must plan to examine and have an impact on policy that promotes educational improvement and equity for students.
- Collaborative efforts must offer evidence of a strong commitment to assess work (Ford Foundation, 1997, p. 2).

The Ford Foundation specified one other condition for undertaking this initiative: sites ultimately would be judged by whether or not their work produced gains in student test scores. As the foundation put it, "the linkage between proposed activities and improving student academic achievement should be clearly drawn" (Ford Foundation, 1997, p. 3). As stated in the RFP, "At the conclusion of the two-year implementation period, successful efforts might be invited to submit new proposals for supplemental funding" (Ford Foundation, 1997, p. 3). The foundation's declared intention was that it would support site work for up to 10 years, assuming progress was evident. Encouraged to think of CERI as a 10-year initiative, this timeframe had the effect of dimming the message heard by sites to make immediate progress.

Finally, while the foundation's RFP emphasized the creation of systemic changes and the need for clear progress, initial meetings between the foundation and sites often did not focus on these two points but rather on professional development, K–12 alignment, and parental involvement. The foundation stated that these foci were the result of the views of the three program officers in charge of CERI—each believing that one of these areas was important to ultimate success. They did not represent a coherent strategy per se. Instead they represented different program officer's own theories of reform. The foundation staff indicated in later interviews that these three areas were further developed in conversations with sites and came to be emphasized in an informal manner. Thus, at least partly in reaction to what they heard, sites reported focusing their interventions on providing additional professional development to the cluster schools and on implementing K–12 alignment activities. Few initially concentrated on the creation of a policy agenda or of systemic reform.

In fact, most proposals submitted by the sites addressed the development and piloting of activities aimed at professional development, K–12 alignment, and parental involvement with little specific guidance for how they would promote systemwide education reform. One reason for this might be that four sites had prior connections to the UPP and because of this were heavily focused on alignment (high school to college alignment being the purpose of the UPP). So much was this the case, that several Ford Foundation program staff were worried that some of the former UPP sites saw the CERI effort as UPP-2.

Profile of the Sites at the Start of CERI

The literature review indicates that initial conditions at sites are important to whether or not collaboratives make progress and to the speed and strength of that progress. This section describes the characteristics of the sites as seen in 1998—the start of this initiative. It is intended to help the reader understand both the complexity and the challenges that sites faced in developing collaboratives in their respective communities. Further detail about each site is included in the appendices.

Initial Membership Rationale
The foundation asked sites to build collaborations that include a broad range of organizations, institutions, and community leaders. The foundation believed that such broad membership would give grantees the ability to push for reform from outside the central office and to incorporate innovations from inside the central office as well.

Differences across sites were evident. Cataño, D.C., Denver, Jackson, and Miami, for example, contained a variety of "outside organizations," including universities and colleges, community-based organizations, and school reform networks. In contrast, Charlotte's and Santa Ana's partnerships were initially less diverse, involving primarily the central office and institutions of higher education.

The former UPP sites, Cataño, Denver, Miami, and Santa Ana, already had partnerships. These collaboratives were largely defined by preexisting networks from the UPP days. In these sites, new partners were not always brought to the table initially; Cataño and Santa Ana did alter the existing partnership to involve new organizations. Each relied heavily on the existing network to support CERI.

Early interviews with members across sites revealed a common process among the newly formed collaboratives for determining who would participate. The foundation had sent the RFP letter to multiple organizations within a community, hoping to instigate their coming together to consider joint work. Organizations that received an RFP from the Ford Foundation and were interested in the proposed initiative did come together—usually with one organization acting as a host for the initial meeting. The group then considered who else from the community should be approached to participate in the endeavor, making decisions based on reputed strengths and interests. In general, potential grantees tended to target organizations or people that they believed would help sell the proposal to the foundation or could help address one of the Ford Foundation's three emphases: pre-K through 12 alignment; professional development; and parent and community engagement.

Through this process of selling the proposal rather than thinking through who was needed to do the work, several grantees ended up with members who would later leave or who had little devotion to the effort. This would result in at least several cases of restructuring in later years as will be described below.

Demographics and Resources

All of the CERI sites were involved in this effort because they shared important characteristics. The sites were in urban areas that served significant percentages of low-income, usually minority, students that had been underserved by the existing school infrastructure. As is common in urban school settings serving low-income students, all the CERI sites reported in interviews or in their proposals to the foundation that their students had lower than desired academic performance and that parental involvement in their children's education was low. In addition, most reported that the high-stakes testing regimes in place or being put in place made the low academic performance of their students a strong public concern. Moreover, the high-stakes testing regime sites tended to report that the accountability mechanisms were driving teachers toward more skill and drill types of pedagogy. This was a cause for concern given that many of the students needed enrichment activities as much as basic skills competence.

Our initial visits to the sites in spring 2000 indicated that contrasts also existed among the sites.

Table 3.2 summarizes the levels of commonality and differences among sites. Arrayed down the side are descriptors of the economic and social characteristics of each site. Unless otherwise noted, these are values for the district or community, not the target cluster. In Cataño, however, the district was small enough that CERI was able to target all of the schools within the district.

First, while the communities in which the sites were located all had pockets of extreme poverty, in fact the level of poverty varied across sites from more than 90 percent of students in Cataño and San Antonio eligible for free and reduced-price lunch (FRL) to 36 percent eligible in Charlotte. Furthermore, the Jackson and Cataño communities were characterized by declining tax bases and increasing poverty levels. It was unlikely that economic growth would fuel a rise in tax revenues to support schools or a rise in income of families in these two communities. In contrast, the Charlotte area was undergoing major economic growth that not only was increasing tax revenues that could be targeted toward schools but was also raising the income of many families as well.

Table 3.2 makes clear that the district or city economy in many cases was better off than the targeted cluster. The collaboratives chose to work in high-poverty areas of their communities. In addition, several targeted clusters were characterized by respondents as being isolated from the larger community. This was often the case because of the layout of highways, lack of transportation, or cultural contrasts.

Some of the sites, but not all, faced a rapid growth in students with limited English proficiency (LEP). LEP rates varied from less than 5 percent of students in Jackson to more than 87 percent in Santa Ana. Those with large numbers of immigrants, such as Santa Ana, Denver, San Antonio, and Miami, struggled to meet the language acquisition needs of these students. Other sites, such as Jackson and Cataño, did not face such challenges.

Several of the sites experienced student population increases and were scrambling to house the rapidly growing student population. In rapid growth areas, such as Miami and Santa Ana, building new schools was a high priority and ate up significant revenues available to the district as well as the administration's time and energy. Oftentimes, districts in these circumstances paid less attention to curriculum and instruction simply because housing their students became a more immediate concern. In contrast, along with their declining tax bases, Jackson and Cataño had a declining student enrollment. The District of Columbia also reported significant declines in enrollment over the past decade.

In summary:

- Jackson and Cataño had large low-income populations, little prospect for economic growth in the surrounding economy and served a declining population that spoke the predominant language.

Table 3.2
Site Characteristics in 1998–1999

	Cataño	Charlotte	Denver	D.C.	Jackson	Miami	San Antonio	Santa Ana
Area economy	Stagnant	Growing	Growing	Growing	Stagnant	Growing	Growing	Growing
Cluster economy	Isolated/stagnant	Growing	Growing/gentrification	Isolated/gentrification	Isolated/stagnant	Stagnant	Isolated/stagnant	Stagnant
Enrollment district/cluster	4,891	97,586/6,375	68,893/2,805	71,889/3,099	31,832/4,786	352,595/11,277	59,080/5,784	56,071/13,236
Students eligible for FRL (%) district/cluster	92	37/58	64/88	68/89	77/91	59/77	87/89	76/76
Limited English proficient district/cluster	Not applicable	4/1	23/43	12/18	None	14/14	17/18	71/75
Student languages	Spanish	English	Bilingual[a]	Multilingual	English	Multilingual	Bilingual[a]	Bilingual[a]

[a]Student population predominantly Spanish-speaking, instruction largely in English.

- Santa Ana, San Antonio, and Miami-Dade, although educating many children from high-poverty backgrounds, had economic growth potential. They were challenged by the demand to address the needs of children speaking languages other than English.
- Denver and D.C. had common traits in that a significant portion of the cluster students were English-speaking African-American and the rest primarily Hispanic immigrants. They were surrounded by strong economies and their respective clusters were being "gentrified." However, this economic boom did not necessarily flow into the families within the cluster schools.
- Charlotte-Mecklenburg had the fewest students from impoverished backgrounds, a strong growth potential, and few students speaking other languages.

District Size, Politics, and Governance

The sites also showed interesting contrasts in terms of the political and governing environment within the district.

Size. The districts differed dramatically in size and in the levels of government needed to administer them. Cataño was the smallest of the districts. The Commonwealth of Puerto Rico had recently passed a law decentralizing its educational governance structure, diminishing the role of the district. At the beginning of this initiative, the schools had started to report directly to the regional offices of the commonwealth. Miami-Dade was the largest district, and the schools reported to the top leadership through a very complex bureaucratic chain. Clearly the sites faced different challenges in attempting to create systemic changes in the central office and to change the behaviors of very different numbers of teachers across the sites.

Superintendent Turnover. The districts associated with the target clusters of CERI had one important characteristic in common. None of the superintendents had been in office for more than four years. However, recent superintendent tenure varied. For example, Jackson had four superintendents in the five years preceding the initiative. In contrast, Charlotte had less turnover. Turnover in this position often resulted in a change to the reform agenda, needed or not. Perhaps the site with the greatest challenges was the District of Columbia, where, after significant superintendent turnover, the public schools were under the control of the federally appointed Financial Control Board at the beginning of the effort.

Racial Inequity. All sites dealt with issues of race-based policies or attempts to eradicate them. For example, Charlotte was the home of the Swann decision, the first federal court-ordered busing of students for desegregation purposes. A federal judge had recently reversed this long-held policy and ordered the district to stop race-based placement of students in schools. This was appealed. As of 1998, the district and courts were going back and forth on this issue. The result was that during our initial site visit respondents reported that the court battle had drained attention from curricular improvements. Moreover, the feelings associated with these struggles for racial equity in schooling had damaged the cohesion of the community. No matter what the outcome of the court decision, the collaborative had much work to do to build community coherence around school reform.

Other sites experienced similar divisions in the past. The target clusters often included areas where parents and teachers felt that the district had not applied resources equitably. Alternatively, Santa Ana was characterized by a divide between the largely Hispanic, English as a second language students who attended its schools and needed significant interventions to help them succeed and the largely white, middle-class voters in the community, as well as across the state, who had not supported tax increases to encourage such efforts.

Challenges Reported by Sites

During our first visits to sites in spring 2000, we asked respondents from the different collaboratives, communities, and schools to describe the educational challenges of their cluster schools. Based on the statements of respondents at all sites, three major challenges emerged as being common among the clusters: low academic performance, low or poor parental involvement, and high numbers of student dropouts. This implied that indeed each site needed serious improvements in teaching and learning in classrooms. Other challenges varied across the sites, with some sites reporting only minor challenges and others reporting major difficulties.

Several sites reported a significant shortage of teachers caused by rapid growth in the student population, class-size reduction policies, large numbers of retirements, or all of these factors together. In some sites, the schools in the target cluster had such poor conditions, real or by repute, that teachers were leaving to move to other schools with better reputations found inside and outside of the district. When teacher mobility was high, respondents said cluster schools were left with a less experienced and less qualified teaching force. Cataño, with its stagnant economy and surplus labor, had almost no teacher turnover. On the other hand, respondents from Charlotte, Denver, the District of Columbia, Miami-Dade, and Santa Ana reported high teacher turnover as well as flight.

In addition, several sites, especially Denver, Miami, and Santa Ana, reported significant challenges in meeting the needs of a growing population of students with English as a second language.

Site Collaboratives

From the beginning, the proposed collaboratives differed in several respects: the number and composition of members, their history, and the nature of the designated lead.

Members of the Collaborative. The numbers of collaborative members varied from as few as four in Cataño to as many as 19 in D.C. They included local colleges and universities, community-based organizations, education and youth related nonprofit organizations, schools, educators, and concerned citizens. In a few cases, collaborative members also included religious and governmental organizations.

Preexistence of the Collaboratives. Some of the collaboratives had long working histories and had had more time to develop smooth pathways for members to communicate and make joint decisions. Newly formed collaboratives had to work out the details of collaboration, including the nature of membership, communication, and decisionmaking. Interorganizational linkages in Charlotte-Mecklenburg, D.C., Jackson, and San Antonio had not existed prior to the initiative and were formed in an effort to respond to the Ford Foundation RFP.

Collaborative Lead. The school district was clearly an organization that CERI desired to influence and change in significant ways. The goals of more coherent professional development, better K–12 alignment, and improved community support hinged on current activities of the district and the collaborative's success in changing them. The assumption of the entire initiative was that the district was at least a part of the problem. It seemed self-evident, therefore, that it had to be part of the solution, but what part?

The Ford Foundation chose sites whose collaboratives involved very different roles for the central office. For example, in Charlotte and Santa Ana the central office served as both the lead and the fiduciary agent of the collaborative. In contrast, in Cataño, the District of Columbia, and Jackson, the role of the central office was comparatively quite diminished in the original proposal. Central office representatives acted as consultants or as one of many representatives around the table. In the three other sites, namely Denver, Miami, and San Antonio, the proposals implied that the district central office was an equal partner among other members. Given the literature on the importance of including major constituencies, it was appropriate to include the district as partner. However, the district as lead was seen as potentially problematic because CERI would then depend on an "inside organization" to guide the reform effort—something each of the sites indicated in their proposals had not worked in the past.

Implications for Expectations

From this description of the sites in 1998, it should be clear that the sites had a great deal in common in terms of low academic achievement for significant numbers of students, including high dropout rates. Each community also faced significant poverty, rapid turnover of superintendents, etc. Each also was marked by contrasting local contexts in terms of demographics, politics, history of collaborative efforts, and political rifts or fragmentations (see appendix). Given these contexts, it was expected that the sites would form somewhat different types of interorganizational linkages, possibly identify different specific problems to address, choose varying methods to address problems, and make dissimilar progress.

Roles of Learning Communities Network and RAND

The Ford Foundation learned from its UPP experience of the usefulness of technical assistance for sites and of the need for strong evaluations of such initiatives. In 1999, the foundation asked the Learning Communities Network (LCN), Inc. of Cleveland, Ohio, to act as the technical assistance provider for the initiative. LCN is a nonprofit entity committed to helping all citizens ensure that their children experience schooling and learning opportunities that enable them to succeed. Just before approaching LCN, the foundation asked RAND to become the evaluator of the effort, stressing that it take a formative assessment approach for the first several years.

From spring 2000 to fall 2000, the first full year of LCN and RAND activity, both took several important actions that helped set the tone for the remainder of the initiative. Both visited the CERI sites: LCN in fall 1999 to set up technical assistance if needed and RAND in spring 2000 to conduct its first round of site visits for the formative evaluation.

Routinely, for four years (school year [SY] 1999–2000, SY 2000–2001, SY 2001–2002, SY 2002–2003), RAND provided both qualitative and quantitative reports to the sites on their individual progress. In addition, at the convenings of all sites, RAND reported on the analyses of cross-site progress and common issues. LCN played a key role in facilitating discussions at these convenings around the issues identified by it and RAND.

In June 2000, the Ford Foundation convened all the sites to hear the initial round of findings from the RAND site visits. RAND presented information, similar to the above description of early site characteristics, which showed the commonalities and differences across the sites at their starting points. In addition, it showed what each site was doing with the clusters in several key areas: creating more coherent professional development, aligning curriculum and

K–12 instruction, and increasing public involvement. RAND findings made clear that all the collaboratives were using foundation funding to directly pay for professional development within the sites. With the exception of Cataño and D.C., most had not focused on the issue of making the system of professional development more coherent or cohesive, as was the goal indicated in the original RFP.

Finally, only one site, D.C., had really attended to the creation of a systemic policy agenda as an activity intended to keep voters and the greater public informed about the education issues in the community. Other sites interpreted policy engagement to mean increasing traditional parental involvement, such as encouraging attendance, ensuring that homework got done, or serving on site-based councils.

In general, RAND noted at this convening, as well as through individual site reports sent to each collaborative, concerns over a lack of review of data to understand the problems within the clusters and sites, lack of strong connections between purported problems and solutions being pursued, and a tendency of sites to use collaborative funds to seemingly substitute for district resources to cover professional development and other activities. Given the small amount of funds provided by Ford for collaboration relative to the very large amounts of funds districts had at their disposal and the availability of federal Title I and Comprehensive School Reform funds for school improvement purposes, this approach seemed unlikely to have much impact. Equally important, it only added professional development activities but did not necessarily address the issue of coherence. Thus, discussion centered around how sites could more usefully employ the funds for creating more systemic change and for building collaboratives, rather than for providing direct services.

The next meeting held for all sites was in December 2000. LCN provided strong support to sites through a series of actions. First, it provided a briefing to all sites on strategic planning and the steps necessary to ensure a viable process. The briefing emphasized the importance of data gathering, proper problem identification, and the needed connection between problems and activities. It stressed that the collaboratives should be focused just as much on terminating unneeded activities within the districts as they were on creating new ones and attempted to help collaboratives understand the concept of slack as a prerequisite to strategic change. In addition, LCN arranged for RAND and the individual collaboratives to meet to promote a sound understanding of the theory of education behind the collaboratives' efforts and their theory of change.

RAND's briefing at this convening covered the results of the spring 2000 survey of all teachers in the cluster schools (average response rates across sites was 62 percent). The complete findings from the teacher survey were reported to Ford and the CERI sites in an internal memorandum, but the briefing made several important points about teacher perceptions that are relevant to the overall findings presented in this report:

- Approximately 90 percent of teachers reported involvement in reform efforts in the past six months. They reported few conflicts between new standards, assessments, curriculum frameworks, and their own efforts at improvement.
- Teachers also reported high rates of participation in professional development activities with 56 percent reporting that these opportunities had improved over the last year and 72 percent reporting that the overall quality of activities was strong.
- In contrast, teachers reported a significant lack of support for improvements in the following areas:
  - On average, about 48 percent reported that they received little support from administrators and other teachers to change their practices.
  - On average, 61 percent of teachers reported that a lack of resources inhibited their ability to implement improved practices. These included insufficient planning time, inadequate classroom materials and facilities, and insufficient time to practice new skills.
  - About one-third to one-half of teachers noted that reforms were transient at their schools. Only 38 percent reported regular follow-up to cement ideas gained from professional development into practice.

— Only 26 percent reported having observed another classroom over the last year.
— About 45 percent of teachers reported very low parental involvement in the schools with the participation levels falling with increasing grade levels. Importantly, while teachers were dissatisfied with involvement levels, 72 percent reported that their school was involved in significant outreach. Most teachers reported traditional means for doing so, such as through newsletters and parent-teacher conferences.

This briefing formed the basis of discussion with all sites about the issue of paying for additional professional development. Teachers had identified lack of follow-through as the primary problem with professional development. The survey results also indicated that some of the collaboratives' traditional approaches to parental involvement had already been tried by teachers and would be unlikely to result in policy changes or public engagement around a policy agenda.

At other convenings over the next two years, RAND continued to emphasize the variable progress of the sites and also several common issues, such as the lack of use of data to understand issues in sites' clusters and districts, while pointing to several examples of cases where sites did use data well; the disconnect between activities and desired goals; and the lack of attention to creating plans for sustainment and scale-up.

Partly in response to this disconnect between problems and the solutions proposed by several collaboratives, the Ford Foundation offered sites the services of LCN to help develop new strategies. The foundation agreed to pay for one-half the costs of the services; sites would be responsible for the other half. In several cases, if sites took advantage of this offer, LCN was able to provide significant resources and facilitation to enable sites to more carefully consider and plan their activities. This appeared to be most especially the case in Cataño, D.C., and Jackson. Each of these sites actively sought the aid of LCN. They later reported that they benefited from interactions with LCN in setting in place a strategic planning process that allowed members to more carefully consider goals, objectives, activities, and progress toward outcomes. Indeed, after several years and with some help from LCN, Cataño, Jackson, and D.C. emerged with clear and logical plans that included well-articulated expectations for progress over time. Miami achieved this without seeking much help from LCN.

In contrast, several sites did not take advantage of this assistance even after some prodding by Ford. The Denver and San Antonio sites, despite several interactions indicating that they were not making progress as expected, seemed especially unresponsive to Ford's advice and urging.

Developing a Set of Common Characteristics for Well-Functioning Collaboratives

The RFP put forward by the Ford Foundation in 1998 listed specific goals it saw as critical to promoting systemic reform and stated that only efforts deemed successful would possibly be invited to submit new proposals for supplemental funding at the conclusion of a two-year period—i.e., the life of each implementation grant. Thus, from the inception of CERI, the foundation had stressed continuous progress in its written communication to the sites, given its acknowledgement that collaboratives were unlikely to achieve the multiple goals it promoted, let alone affect student achievement, within two years.

The dialogue between the foundation and the sites had not always been clear on what was meant by systemic change. Oftentimes, the notion of parental involvement activities within the cluster were confused with the community involvement campaign that the foundation attempted to encourage. In addition, the scale-up of specific cluster activities to other schools outside the feeder pattern—e.g., a professional development program in math, was talked about as systemic reform.

By the second year of the initiative, the end of the first cohort's implementation grant in July 2001, the foundation staff were feeling some frustration with the sites in that not all were making the progress for which the staff had hoped. Moreover, the expectation of a systemic policy agenda seemed not to have been heard. In addition, the formation of strong interorganizational linkages was not apparent in all sites. Thus, the foundation, with assistance from RAND and LCN, developed a set of common criteria it called "elements of success" against which progress could be judged. The literature and the review of site contexts pointed to the need for variable expectations. Indeed in the early years of the effort, the sites claimed that they should not be compared to each other because of their differences. However, the foundation thought that these differences did not preclude a set of common expectations toward progress. It indicated that progress would likely vary for very good reasons across sites. Thus, a set of indicators of success was developed and provided to the sites during the fall convening of 2001 (see Table 3.3). The foundation chose to emphasize the elements of success and provide clarity to the sites at this convening, given the possibility that mixed messages had been heard in the past.

Discussion at the fall convening concerned the need for sites to focus on building strong collaboratives and on affecting policy. The foundation took the opportunity again to try to make clear that it expected progress or it would not re-fund sites. Some collaborative members expressed concern that the foundation's decision to tie-off funding to some sites was an unfair increase in expectations, having understood the foundation's original references to a 10-year initiative to mean that sites had 10 years to demonstrate impact.

Second Round and Actions in Spring 2003

Further interactions between the foundation and the sites over the next several years emphasized and clarified further what was meant by scale-up of cluster activities, systemic policy changes, and sustainment of the efforts. In particular, discussions at the February 2002 convening in Dallas, Texas, helped to clarify a point regarding the meaning of sustainment. Specifically, sustainment as used in Table 3.3 was confusing. Thus, two different meanings were made clear:

Table 3.3
Elements of Success Proposed by Ford Foundation—November 2001

A functioning collaborative is in place
— Collaboratives have diverse membership, the composition is somewhat dependent on the strategy selected

Members work together collaboratively as evidenced by the following types of behaviors or outcomes:
- Effective leadership that moves the collaborative forward
- All members buy in to the purpose of the collaborative and its activities
- Each partner meets its unique responsibilities
- The collaborative practices group decisionmaking around a collective strategy
- Synergistic effects accrue
- Benefits of joint action accrue to all partners.

The collaborative implements a vision of quality teaching leading to improved student experiences and outcomes
— The collaborative develops a clearly articulated statement of unifying purpose centered on improving instructional practice, curricula, and student outcomes
— It has specific plans and activities indicating a coherent theory of change that connect activities to desired outcomes
— The activities are consistent with the values of the foundation
— The collaborative executes its plans and shows evidence of progress toward its vision.

The collaborative implements a clear strategy for sustainment of its work at a broader scale
— It has a clearly articulated strategy
— It has developed specific plans
— It executes the strategy and shows evidence toward sustainment.

The collaborative actions help lead to improved student experiences and outcomes, including
— Improved student achievement
— More coherent and collegial professional development
— Increased parental support for reforms in school and for improving public education
— Improvement in systemic or policy capacity.

- The foundation expected all sites to eventually become independent of it. In this way, sustainment was used to indicate that the sites should sustain themselves over time.
- Sustainment also referred to the policy agenda. The idea here was that the cluster activities could not be sustained without significant changes in the policy environment. The foundation made clear that it expected all sites to develop a policy agenda

and push it forward to support and sustain improved classroom practices.

In 2001 and 2002, depending on the cohort, the foundation asked sites to submit new proposals for funding and announced that only a subset of sites would be awarded additional grants. The foundation emphasized in this announcement that it was moving toward a new phase of CERI with heavier emphasis on public engagement, sustainment, and scale-up. It would look for progress in this direction, including some indication that sites were thinking about ways to fund their efforts without continued dependence on the foundation.

Several sites took great exception to the notion of financial independence stating that the foundation had guaranteed funding for 10 years and that the level of progress it was looking for was unfounded. Other sites were not interested in pursuing the policy agenda being pushed by the foundation and wanted to continue with their cluster work, at least for the time being.

All sites submitted proposals. The Ford Foundation's final decisions were based on the substance of sites' proposals, RAND's interim reports, LCN's informal feedback, and the foundation's own visits. Heavy emphasis was placed on the progress that sites had made toward a policy agenda and toward their own sustainment. In some cases, progress simply entailed moving from a position that denied these as important to agreeing that these were important concerns.

In 2003, the Ford Foundation announced that it would continue funding only three of the eight sites (Cataño, D.C., and Jackson). Four were to receive "tie-off funding"—i.e., a limited amount of funding to complete the work described in their most recent proposals (Denver, Miami-Dade, San Antonio, and Santa Ana). Charlotte remained an anomalous case, receiving funding but with strong warning from the foundation to improve its efforts.

In August 2002, the foundation awarded planning grants to three additional sites: Austin, Texas; Chicago, Illinois; and Philadelphia, Pennsylvania. In August 2003, Austin and Chicago became a part of the second phase of CERI. RAND did not collect information from the three new planning grant sites and began working only recently (winter 2003) to bring the two new sites into the CERI evaluation.

Implications

The intent of this chapter was to provide an overview of the emerging initiative—focusing on the relationship between the foundation and the sites and including details of their original conditions. Several themes stood out and need to be considered in judging progress. They could also be useful to other foundations considering these types of efforts.

This effort clearly was developmental in many senses, but most especially in the understanding between the sites and the foundation as to goals and expectations. The alignment of goals between the Ford Foundation and specific sites was somewhat problematic and led to several slow starts.

The Ford Foundation asked sites to promote the following at the cluster level: more coherent professional development, the development of parental involvement, and better K–12 alignment. The foundation also talked in unclear terms about the systemic impact and policy changes it hoped to achieve. Sites heard this message and interpreted it in different ways. Later, Ford voiced dissatisfaction with site progress and clarified its meanings and expectations through briefings, convenings, phone calls, and conferences. This greater clarity was helpful to some sites. Others still did not "get it."

While this theme of the development of clearer goals and expectations applies to the relationship between the foundation and the sites, it also applies to the foundation. It could be said that the foundation itself learned over time what the initiative was really about and consequently clarified its goals.

In addition, the effort, or at least some sites, clearly benefited from the technical assistance provided by LCN. It is in fact those sites that took greatest advantage of this assistance, and were especially helped in thinking strategically about systemic change, that produced second-round proposals accepted by Ford.

Briefings, memos, convenings and other types of forums that encouraged interactions and exchange of data and views among and between the sites, the foundation, and the technical assistance provider all proved fruitful in moving the effort forward and became an important contributor toward its evolution.

Finally, the work of an organization, such as RAND, that provides objective analysis of progress was important in supporting the conversations needed by the parties involved and by providing concrete information on which to base decisions.

Thus, we conclude that several practices emerged from the initiative that could prove useful to others, including significant work and devotion to clarifying and effectively communicating goals and expectations, the use of technical assistance providers to help improve the understanding of the sites, the use of multiple forums for interaction among all involved parties, and the use of a separate neutral party to collect data on progress. All these helped move the evolution and development of this effort forward from tentative beginnings to more concrete understandings.

CHAPTER FOUR

Progress of Sites

In the last chapter, we discussed the relationships between the foundation and the sites and overall progress made toward achieving a clearer understanding of goals and providing support to sites in achieving those goals.

This chapter presents the progress of the sites compared to each other using the set of indicators developed in Chapter Two. As should be clear from Chapter Three, the sponsor did not have an absolute standard by which to judge progress. Therefore, to assess progress, we compared a grantee's level of development to other grantees as well as to the levels of progress found in the literature. At the same time, we recognize that sites each operated within unique circumstances and faced different constraints. Therefore, we note equal progress should not be expected.

In addition, even if a collaborative had developed, planned for, and implemented a set of activities geared to improve the quality of teaching and learning in the cluster, established a policy agenda, and established and implemented plans for sustainment, these might not have translated into impacts on outcomes. Contextual factors might have interfered with impacts, or the theory of education behind the set of implemented activities might have been flawed. Either case could have been identified by grantees if a system of assessment and feedback was in place and utilized to improve their respective practices. In these cases, one would have expected the sites to be aware of any shortfall and to develop new interventions to improve potential impacts.

Overview of Site Progress

As of spring 2003, no site had accomplished all that it set out to do at the inception of CERI, but some had made stronger, more encouraging progress than others in achieving their respective visions. The following assessment is summarized in Table 4.1.

- All of the grantees developed networks to share information and to act cooperatively with each other.
- Four of the eight grantees, those in Cataño, D.C., Jackson, and Miami, made comparatively strong progress toward the formation of collaborative linkages. Santa Ana created a well-functioning partnership to garner additional grant money for routine activities. San Antonio, too, created a well-functioning partnership but functioned largely to coordinate the multiple activities of the various member organizations. Grantees in Denver and Charlotte made weaker progress in the development of organizational linkages. While they maintained network linkages, they struggled to build shared visions and/or to create joint operations or products through spring 2003.
- Although never fully implementing all planned cluster activities that addressed improved teaching and learning, five grantees contributed to the development and implementation of visions of high-quality teaching and supports in their locales (Cataño, D.C., Jackson, Miami, and Santa Ana). Three of these, Cataño, Jackson, and Santa Ana, moved toward expansion of several cluster-level activities to other schools, either within the district or to other schools within the area. Charlotte, Denver, and San Antonio, each with less-developed organizational linkages, made weaker progress toward implementation at least in part because members did not agree on the vision or the vision was not central to improving teaching and learning, or they did not pool their resources to implement the agreed on vision.
- Three of the grantees, those in Cataño, D.C., and Jackson made progress toward policy changes and/or toward expanding policy

Table 4.1
Overview of Progress as of Spring 2003

Level of Progress	Charlotte	Denver	San Antonio	Santa Ana	Jackson	Miami	Cataño	D.C.
Create inter-organizational linkages	Network	Network	Coordinating partnership	Coordinating partnership	Collaborative	Collaborative	Collaborative	Collaborative
Cluster-level activities	Piloting a few activities in a few schools	Planning, constant revisions	Inconsistently implemented, but decline in last year caused by funding shortfalls	Implemented many, expanded two	Piloting most, implementing council concept	Implementing, with some dropped due to funding shortfalls	Expanding program into five districts	Implementing
Systemic Policy Activities	Planning	Planning	Planning	Planning many, implementing a few	Piloting	Not included	Planning	Implementing
Sustainment	Planning	Planning	Planning	Matched funds, but now directed to non-CERI work	Planning	Planning	Significant	Significant
Improved outcomes	Weak	Weak	Weak	Moderate	Weak	Moderate	Moderate	Moderate

influence. The collaborative in Miami-Dade did not see its work in terms of systemic change and did not move deliberately toward ensuring districtwide support of changes to policies outside. Four grantees, Charlotte, Denver, San Antonio, and Santa Ana, were at the planning stages of policy development.

- Cataño and D.C. took significant steps toward sustaining the collaborative and its CERI focus through a combination of opportunistic and deliberate actions. Santa Ana also took steps to bring in significant grant funding, but this was directed toward other initiatives. Others were in the planning stages or had perhaps drawn in some minor funding supports.

- Very little improvement on student achievement attributable to the grantees was made across most sites. Jackson, Miami, and Santa Ana, however, might be credited with some test score increases. On the other hand, interim organizational results were evident across more sites but depended greatly on the action plans and conditions there.

Four Types of Experiences Emerged

As can be seen in Table 4.1 we arranged the sites across the horizontal axis in a different order than we had previously. As we listened to interviewees in different sites and analyzed the data, it became clear that the sites clustered into three types of experiences that captured the level of progress and much of the explanation for it. Two sites, Charlotte and Denver, created struggling partnerships that still faced significant challenges to the viability of a collaborative. Activities sometimes changed yearly. Two other sites, San Antonio and Santa Ana, made more significant progress but tended to treat the CERI effort as a source of funding directed at the target cluster for partners' existing or routine activities. Cluster activities showed little indication of joint action or joint benefits and both sites made little progress toward policy changes. The four remaining sites, Cataño, D.C., Jackson, and Miami, reached a collaborative level of functioning and developed and implemented cluster activities through joint action.

While Jackson and Miami made moderate progress toward expansion, sustainment, and policy changes, D.C. and Cataño made more notable progress in these areas. Within this initiative, these two offered the strongest examples of progress toward goals. No sites progressed strongly toward both cluster-level activities and systemic policy change.

The next sections provide a brief history of each of the collaboratives organized into these four groupings: struggling partnerships, coordinated partnerships, collaboratives with moderate progress, and collaboratives with significant progress. More detailed descriptions of individual sites are included in the appendices.

Struggling Partnerships

Two sites, Charlotte and Denver, did not exhibit as significant a level of progress as the other sites in part because each struggled with the first step of the process: creating a shared vision among partners and creating a governance and leadership structure that brought the partners together. These two sites seldom implemented the other components as the partners struggled to define roles and responsibilities that would enable the partnership to flourish.

Charlotte
Charlotte-Mecklenburg Schools had an enrollment of about 97,600 students at the start of this effort. The Charlotte site did not have a functioning collaborative prior to this effort. On receipt of the RFP in 1998, the Charlotte-Mecklenburg Education Foundation, with strong network links to the other recipients, convened those who had received invitations to discuss how to respond to the RFP. The response to the RFP was led by the foundation. Near the moment of submittal, a change in leadership at the foundation and the resulting turnover of several staff left it unable to take on a strong leadership role. Members met and decided to give the central office of the Charlotte-Mecklenburg Schools the lead, specifically the regional superintendent who oversaw the chosen feeder pattern, West-

Mecklenburg. Of all the member organizations, it was seen as having the capacity and means to take on this role.

The West-Mecklenburg cluster with about 6,300 students was known to be the poorest cluster in the district. The plan was for a director to be appointed who would report directly to the regional superintendent. The seven original partners would sit on an advisory board to provide advice to the director. They included

- Charlotte-Mecklenburg Public Schools
- Charlotte-Mecklenburg Education Foundation
- Public School Forum of North Carolina
- North Carolina Education and Law Center
- Central Piedmont Community College
- Johnson C. Smith University
- University of North Carolina at Charlotte.

Activities developed by the partners would be presented to a newly formed Principals' Council. The principals from the cluster would determine what was to be implemented and what was not. The regional superintendent would call meetings of the principals on a regular basis.

The proposal emphasized activities geared toward school improvement, including student achievement, parental involvement, higher-education links, high expectations, and school reform models. The school reform models were chosen by the director and regional superintendent without much input from principals or the other partnership members. Much of the work was targeted at elementary schools in the system and the majority of early activities were dedicated to paying for teachers' staff development on reform models in the cluster schools. For example, the collaborative paid for teachers' and principals' staff development on both the Comer and High-Reliability Schools models. Given that these came from vendor organizations, no joint development of activities was involved. In another part of the effort, the director, whose salary was subsidized by the grant, identified and brought together master teachers within the cluster to discuss their best practices. This resulted in the identification of 13 practices that the collaborative wanted all schools in the feeder area to adopt. The director and others reported, however, that little happened in terms of implementation after the practices were identified. Disagreement apparently arose within the group about who should present the practices to schools. One collaborative member explained that instead of trying to work through this issue, the process simply "broke down because of the inability to get along." As for activities around K–12 alignment and community engagement, including parent involvement, all remained largely in the planning stages.

While the activities were directed at the cluster level, not all principals committed to the initiative. Many suggested in early interviews that without the regional superintendent requiring their participation in the collaborative, they would not have been involved in CERI. Many expressed dismay with the interaction between the district and the collaborative, saying that the communication between the two was poor. The strong oversight role of the central office had evolved into a top-down decisionmaking process not readily discernable as separate from the other district policies, thus dampening buy-in from the principals. Other principals felt disengaged because they were interested in addressing issues of more immediate concern, such as their school's improvement efforts in North Carolina's high-stakes testing regime. Capturing the sentiments of many, one principal stated, "Our plates are so full. There are too many things pulling our time." Moreover, principals expressed frustration that even after much time had passed, still no consensus had been reached in terms of a plan for what the principals would do together. In fact, some tension surfaced within the group because the principals of the high school and middle schools believed their issues to be different from those of the elementary schools and thus found little from the meetings to take back to their buildings.

Partners from the institutions of higher education never got involved in the initiative to the extent intended. As the cluster principals did, the different representatives of the higher-education institutions struggled to work as a team. The group decided that it would match students to the services its institutions provided but had a difficult time developing a workable plan for this idea. Some reported that they did not see how they could effectively contribute to the initiative, noting that the partners "functioned more as an advisory board than a collaborative." Other members indicated that, "the members [were] not problem solving; they [did] not act as if they owned the problem." Indeed, given that much emphasis was on improving elementary schools, several higher-education members reported feeling unengaged. Other than the time members gave to attend meetings, their contributions were limited. Two members, the Public School Forum and the North Carolina Education and Law Center were never actively involved in the initiative and were seldom represented at meetings.

Over the next several years, the Charlotte grantees attempted to recover from this start, with a major restructuring at the end of the 2001–2002 school year that led in theory to the inclusion of principals, parents, and representatives from the Chamber of Commerce on the steering committee. Prior to this, the business community in Charlotte, a set of very strong actors in local education improvement, had not been involved. At this time, the Public School Forum and the Law Center, with their roles remaining unclear, were officially removed as members.

In addition, after conducting its first systematic review of data, new goals were chosen. The partnership recognized that it needed to develop a sharper focus. It had set more than 10 goals and pursued a variety of activities to support them. Data indicated that the cluster suffered from significant turnover of teachers and leaders and heavy reliance on inexperienced teachers. Thus, the professional development provided in the first year often went toward training teachers who were likely to leave the schools. The members agreed to change the focus of the collaborative solely to the recruitment and retention of quality teachers and leaders. This also happened to be in keeping with new initiatives by the central office.

New activities were developed for implementation, including coordination of a funding plan to expand a mentoring program for teachers new to West Mecklenburg schools, tuition payments for teachers who chose to pursue a master's degree or a doctoral degree, staff development on cognitive coaching, administrative support for lateral-entry teachers, a Leadership Development Council, and a Teacher Keeper program piloted in two schools.

In summer 2002, both the regional superintendent and the collaborative director left their positions for unrelated reasons and thus dropped from the effort. This left a vacuum at the center of the initiative. Almost by default, the partners chose a different leadership structure than the top-down style that had previously been in place. Two members would lead. One from the business community led the development of cluster activities and the other, a consultant to the effort, served as administrator.

In the last two years of the project, the activities for the cluster were often not hammered out until January or February, leaving only a few months of the school year for implementation. Some activities were not implemented well, given underfunding and/or poor thought about who should receive collaborative-sponsored programs. For example, implementation of the mentoring program was delayed until Ford funds were available in late October. When implemented, the reporting hierarchy of the mentor was unclear, leading to difficulties among mentors, principals, and those being mentored.

Interviews in spring 2003 revealed that the higher-education institutions still did not consider themselves heavily involved. Furthermore, principals continued to indicate that they were not committed to the initiative. With the exception of two principals, they still preferred to spend more time in their schools attempting to meet standards and less time in collaborative activities. Parental attendance at meetings was low. The two current leaders, while sure progress had been made, were less sure of where the partnership was headed and who would be involved. While both now reported that the effort had clearer focus, neither thought that the governance structure was quite right. Members were still struggling in spring 2003 with how to pull the collaborative together. They had planned for neither how to proceed as a collaborative, how to develop a policy agenda, nor how to sustain the types of efforts they were backing.

In terms of student outcomes, over the last five years, the West-Mecklenburg cluster posted increases in tests scores that exceeded the average state and district gains. It also saw improvements in high school completion rates. Thus, something was going on in these schools that translated into improved performance. Given the nature of the interventions implemented by the collaborative, we judged that a prima facie case could not be made for the collaborative having contributed significantly to these results. We note that many of these schools received additional funding through the district's Equity Plus program. Additionally, the district also placed math and literacy coordinators in these schools.

Denver

The Denver Public Schools had an enrollment of about 68,800 at the beginning of this effort. Denver was one of the original UPP sites, and the foundation had invited it to submit a proposal for CERI in 1998. Representatives from the Denver Education Network (DEN) and Public Education and Business Coalition (PEBC) worked on the proposal. The superintendent at the time insisted that the central office shepherd this effort and hired a grant writer to create the proposal without seeking significant input from other groups. The finished product resembled typical grant requests for funding and did not address the collaboration issues that were the basis of CERI. The foundation chose not to fund the proposal.

In the second distribution of the CERI RFP, Denver was again invited to apply. This time, PEBC and DEN led the proposal-writing process. They pulled together a proposal and went to the district to gain its buy-in at the last minute. Matters became confused when two different feeder patterns in the district expressed interest in CERI. DEN had accepted the former UPP schools from the westside cluster as part of the initiative. Meanwhile PEBC had accepted the eastside cluster. The westside principals perceived CERI primarily as a continuation to previous DEN efforts under UPP. The group of principals on the eastside articulated a slightly better understanding of the work but were also motivated by the funds that would be flowing to them for school improvements. The proposed set of activities included professional development, with a particular focus on writing practices; a public engagement campaign to be developed by a team; a team that would learn more about how data could be used more effectively to improve schools; and a policy team. The Ford Foundation approved the proposal with the understanding that PEBC would serve as lead and fiduciary agent for the grant. Despite the planning period and two proposal tries, the different partners had not been involved in a strong effort to share information, goals, or plans and had not developed a strong collective sense of the initiative.

The original partners were

- PEBC
- Denver Public Schools
- Denver Classroom Teachers Association
- DEN
- Cross City Campaign for Urban School Reform
- Latin American Research and Service Agency
- Community College of Denver
- Metro State College of Denver
- University of Colorado at Denver.

After the award of the grant, the leaders of the partner organizations assigned a director to the effort. They hired, through PEBC, a former high school teacher inexperienced in this type of work. At the same time, leaders of the partners stepped away from the grant and designated less-senior individuals from their organizations to serve as representatives to the collaborative. Because the work team members were a set of people different from the original grant writers, many had little understanding of Ford's intentions and lacked buy-in to the proposal. While the director called meetings, they reportedly often involved a great deal of talking, arguments over fund distribution, finger pointing, and arm waving. There was not much in the way of progress toward a solid joint agenda. The inexperienced director lacked the capacity and legitimacy to pull the groups together, and the original leaders were not involved in supporting him. The work groups who met could not find common ground on which to proceed. For example, the preference of principals clashed with the community organizations because the principals wanted the Ford funding to be distributed directly to schools. The situation was further complicated when the original point person for the district was promoted and no one was assigned as a replacement. Thus, no entree into the central office existed.

Unfortunately, the partners never established a strong plan for proceeding in part because of their very poor start. The data development, policy work, and public campaign never moved past planning and piloting for lack of understanding and leadership. By the 2000–2001 school year, the schools recognized the lack of progress and were losing interest in the work. Faced with fading interest and lack of directional support to address the problem, the director made a strategic decision to restructure the partnership by bringing the initiative back to the school level. He solicited input from the principals, composed memorandum outlining the suggested changes, and distributed it to all the partners for feedback. He got none. In response, the director took the initiative and began distributing Ford funds to school teams in the form of minigrants. Although the new approach led to increased attention from the schools, it was at the expense of fostering relationships among the partners and a thoughtful approach to reform. The work in Denver was no longer collaborative or aimed at systemic change.

At the end of the 2000–2001 school year, the project director stepped down and several partners left the effort. A new partner joined the collaborative from the Donnell Kay Foundation. In 2001–2002, in an effort to revive the effort, the executive director of PEBC became more directly involved as did an assistant superintendent of schools and a program officer of the Donnell Kay Foundation. However, their participation lasted only a year. With the planned departure of the foundation program officer for personal reasons and the interest of the assistant superintendent waning, the collaborative once again struggled to develop its purpose in the fourth year. A new chief operating officer of the partnership was appointed and the effort was renamed the NorthEast School Collaborative with a new set of partners. Six teams were formed to develop plans. In general, however, the partners typically made decisions about activities too late in the school year to be implemented and each year a new construct for the collaborative was tried. The partners as a group showed few signs of strategic planning capability. The situation in Denver could only be described as a flailing attempt at collaboration, with members unable to figure out how to work together, not communicating effectively with one another and all stakeholders, not using data, not creating joint activities, and eventually giving significant amounts of the grant funds directly to the schools in a misguided effort to get them interested.

During the five-year period studied, student outcomes in the cluster remained fairly static with the exception of one or two schools. We note that this site had significant changes in testing instruments so judgments were hard to make. Regardless, the partnership's activities were never implemented to an extent that could have contributed to stronger performance.

Reflections

The experiences of these two sites reflected some of the findings from existing literature on the difficulties of establishing a collaborative effort where either the history of such efforts is poor (as in Charlotte) and where leaders with the skills to move partners from information-sharing toward joint visions, activities, and benefits are lacking (as in both Charlotte and Denver). While many other conditions at work in the schools were challenging to overcome, in fact, these partnerships did not really get to the point where these challenges might be relevant. The history of efforts in the direction of collaboration had not provided the handhold for these attempts. Although Denver was a former UPP site, the legacy of that was actually detrimental—some partners and the schools did not understand the new initiative and simply wanted to continue as before. Thus, experiences with UPP did not automatically lead to strong collaboration. Furthermore, leaders treated the initiative in large part as traditional grant making and did not have the wherewithal to bring the diverse partners together.

Also at both, school personnel, teachers, and principals had not taken an active part in the work and had not been engaged in discussions of issues, solutions, the ongoing initiatives, etc. This had two implications. The first is that these sites failed to progress because they did not actively engage the school-level partners. The second is that some of the activities undertaken appeared to be unwarranted and undesired, a situation that might have changed had the school personnel been more actively involved.

While the foundation and RAND encouraged both these sites to seek help in strategic planning and in the development of plans for scale-up, systemic policy approaches, and sustainment, neither site chose to pursue this. Without some outside intervention of this kind, the partner relationships remained the same and little overall progress was made.

Coordinated Partnerships

Two other sites made more significant progress toward interorganizational linkages, and one implemented and expanded a portion of its proposed activities. However, these two sites—San Antonio and Santa Ana—could not be said to have moved toward collaborative functioning. Both used CERI to carry out many existing or routine activities undertaken by the member organizations. For the most part, the activities implemented were not joint efforts with shared products. Santa Ana made more significant headway with policy initiatives.

San Antonio

The San Antonio Public Schools had an enrollment of about 59,000 students at the beginning of this effort. San Antonio was not a former UPP site. The members of this partnership, with the exception of the school district, were familiar to the Ford Foundation from other grant-making activities in the San Antonio area. Each member had a very strong history of working with the largely Hispanic community in San Antonio and was part of an informal network well known to one another. Each nondistrict member came to the initial meetings with a strong history of work in the area and previously developed programs geared toward increasing students' motivation for greater educational attainment, and/or providing educational and social support to students from low-income, primarily Hispanic families in Texas. The members were originally convened by the Intercultural Development Research Association. The district sent very high-level attendees.

The original partners were

- Intercultural Development Research Association
- San Antonio Independent School District
- Alamo Community College District
- Communities Organized for Public Service
- Mexican American Legal Defense and Educational Fund
- University of Texas at San Antonio.

All the partners quickly coalesced around a shared vision articulated in 2000 as creating a seamless network or system that improves student achievement and increases college enrollment and completion. Some initial work in the form of focus groups with teachers, students, community members, and parents was conducted to learn about conditions within the cluster schools, but what they heard was familiar to them, given each of their experiences in the cluster schools and/or community. While the members had a common vision focused on motivating and informing parents and students in the largely low-income, Hispanic community targeted, the agreed on activities tended to enable each partner to carry out its existing program intervention within the cluster schools. The chosen cluster was the Burbank feeder patter with an enrollment of 5,784 students. Workgroups were formed in the following areas: professional development, school-to-school transitions, school-to-college transitions, community engagement, and policy. Each member was responsible for a different work group and tended to work in parallel with the others.

By the end of the 2000–2001 school year, a few activities had been piloted, but many remained in the planning stages. Piloted activities tended to be those already developed by collaborative members. For example, the community college sponsored a "career day" and a transition day for seniors. In later years, it held "Adopt a Hallway" days and sponsored "college graduate" speakers. The sponsor also provided these activities to numerous other schools in the area as part of its outreach. In another example, another set of activities sponsored by the community engagement workgroup annually convened two parent groups to receive leadership training over several months. At meetings, parents were given information about their rights within the educational system and encouraged to ask for their child's school records and access other types of assistance. Again this was an activity that had been developed prior to the formation of the San Antonio collaborative. The school-to-school transition group attempted to engage the teachers from each school in cross-site dialogues about transitions and expectations for students as they were promoted to higher grades. Occasionally, the group also provided speakers to talk about standards and assessments. The policy and professional development groups moved very little beyond the planning stages. In the case of professional development activities, some were implemented over the years but never consistently from one year to the next.

In interviews, each member tended to express its own organization's goals as that of the collaborative. Relations were cordial and the lead organization acted effectively as convener. The San Antonio collaborative divided the Ford funds equally among the members. With the exception of the district, they met as a group throughout the grant period primarily to update each other on progress. Interviewees indicated that after the initial round of meetings, school staff or district representatives had spotty attendance and did not partake fully of the opportunities provided. In part, this stemmed from continuing personnel changes taking place in the district and significant other burdens the district staff were undertaking in a high-stakes testing regime. While cooperation and coordination were apparent in targeting the individual member's activities to the cluster schools, little of the effort could be called joint. Rather, it was characterized by parallel activities.

Unfortunately, over time the partnership showed little evidence of deepening. One partner failed to provide services and eventually was dropped from collaborative when the leadership of that partnering organization turned over. No attempt was made to replace it or to find alternative sources for the provision of those services that had been argued in the proposal as essential to the effort. Over time, the few services that could have directly impacted teachers—e.g., planning across the grades—became redundant with district- and state-level activities and were dropped. In addition, personnel replacement among the partners and within the schools themselves possibly prevented deeper bonds between the schools and the partners and among the partners themselves. While the lead organization remained the same, other turnover was significant. Despite being recommended to do so by the foundation and RAND, the site partners did not take advantage of the technical assistance offered by LCN.

Over time, the impression left by the partners was that they viewed the cluster as simply one more site to which all could provide a set of existing services. The collaborative could neither demonstrate that its activities deepened in implementation within the cluster nor did they expand to other sites after being demonstrated in the Burbank cluster. With regard to the latter, the partners did not keep strong records to justify their impact in order to convince others of their effectiveness.

While the initial vision included making a policy shift, the exact nature of this shift did not develop until the Ford Foundation notified the site that it would tie-off its funding. At that point, the partners met and proposed that the remaining funds be used to develop a set of indicators that could be used by the community to assess the performance of schools. By spring 2003, members reported meeting once to further this goal and could show little concrete work toward its completion.

On average, students in the cluster made gains in test scores that exceeded the district and state averages over the last five years. However, partner activities did not focus on this area. The activities might have been expected, had they been strongly implemented, to increase such course taking as algebra I and completion rates. Over the CERI time period, algebra course taking improved at only one of the cluster schools. High school completion rates did not show a clear change in direction.

Santa Ana

Santa Ana Public Schools had an enrollment of about 56,000 students at the beginning of this effort. Santa Ana Networks had developed as a partnership under the UPP and was seen as one of the most successful sites. Led by two strong personalities from two local colleges, the UPP partners had developed routine meetings and interactions to ensure that the area was successful in bringing in significant grant funding for improvement, seen as absolutely necessary in a predominately poor California district under Proposition 13 prohibitions to raise taxes. These partners routinely called community-based organizations together to jointly plan how to approach major RFPs to successfully bring in funds. Fiduciary responsibility was often rotated so that funds went to different partners. This partnership, with constantly changing scope, exists today and still brings in substantial grant funds to the social and educational reforms in the city of Santa Ana.

Receipt of the Ford RFP quickly mobilized the leads into action convening different partners to respond. The partners were

- Santa Ana Networks—a group of organizations dedicated to improving the educational chances of all Santa Ana citizens
- Santa Ana Unified School District
- Santa Ana College
- University of California at Irvine
- University of California at Riverside
- California State University at Fullerton
- Parent Advisory Council
- Orange County Department of Child and Family Services
- Bilingual District Advisory Council.

Understanding that CERI was different from the UPP, the district was brought in as a partner and became the fiduciary agent for the proposal. With leadership from the district, Santa Ana quickly focused on the new superintendent's Above the Mean initiative as the vehicle for moving forward. This initiative addressed the poor student performance on California standardized tests in math and English.

Santa Ana Networks adopted Above the Mean as its CERI name and dedicated significant portions of the CERI grant to support the professional development needed within the district to implement several new English and math curriculum and instructional models. In the planning year, the partners explored multiple different models to adopt, reviewed literature on best practices in professional development, and used past evaluative data to understand the effectiveness of alternative models before choosing the three it would test. The idea was to determine which worked best and then adopt it district wide. This was to be enabled by the creation of a principal council run by the area superintendent who was also designated the lead for the effort. Other funds, some from matching grants, were dedicated to parental involvement activities and direct student supports, such as a Saturday Math Academy.

In addition, the Santa Ana Networks continued its partnership work in other areas with considerable funds from sources other than the Ford Foundation. CERI could be seen as a part of its larger strategy to improve the educational opportunities and outcomes of all citizens.

Upon receipt of the grant, the partners used a significant portion of Ford Foundation funds to pay for teachers' staff development provided by outside vendors. They focused on three different models to improve English and math instruction in the schools. While very consistent with the Above the Mean initiative of the district, it could not be deemed as a set of joint activities or products developed by the partners. Rather, the majority of funds were passed through to schools to pay for improvement programs.

Implementation was not without some problems. For example, one of the vendor programs was too costly to implement across all the schools and so was confined to a demonstration in a few. Implementation of another program did not go well because of teacher turnover or the failure to find a cohort of teachers interested in undertaking the new training. One vendor program appeared successful but could not be adopted quickly because the vendor did not have the number of trainers needed to supply all the schools. Thus, the partners ended up not using all of their available funding as planned.

The site took an opportunistic approach to the creation of policy changes. During this period, the district adopted the single successful literacy program, originally funded by CERI professional development funds, across all schools. On the other hand the math program and associated professional development funded by CERI were not adopted, in part because they were not consonant with a large textbook adoption by the board. Neither the disciplinary nor the management programs were adopted because of their expense.

Also in this time frame, the district adopted the high school graduation eligibility requirements for acceptance in the university system and adopted a policy establishing seventh-grade pre-algebra and eighth-grade algebra as the academic standard for all students. The latter was an early adoption of a future state mandate requiring all students to take gatekeeper math classes. These changes were claimed to be a result of CERI, but it was difficult to understand the exact connection.

In the 2002–2003 school year, after being told that it would receive tie-off of funds, the Santa Ana Partners (a name change) moved onto other issues in the community and pursued new grants. The two college leads showed impressive ability to maintain the network of partners and move them forward into new grant-writing endeavors. Santa Ana Partners still exists as a fully functioning partnership. However, the CERI initiative does not continue in a recognizable form.

During the course of this study, average test scores in some schools increased at rates above the district and state rate of gain. These increases could partially be a result of the staff development interventions of the partners and indeed in some cases the program implementation and the test score gains aligned. In other cases they did not. High school completion rates increased modestly and algebra course-taking increased significantly. The latter, along with increases in math test scores, could be a prima facie case that the Saturday Math Academy was a success. Both hypotheses could be tested using data on student attendance in the academy, attendance at teacher staff development, and student test scores. However, the partners did not collect this attendance data.

Reflections

Together, these two cases show the difficulties of moving existing networks into new patterns of thinking. Neither provided evidence of significant changes in teaching and learning in classrooms stemming from their interventions. Neither challenged existing relationships and structures to push forward a systemic policy agenda initiative. In the end, both benefited from the funding but primarily in terms of maintaining discretionary funds for their work, not in developing the types of collaboratives that the Foundation wanted or in addressing fundamental issues facing their sites.

In addition, the San Antonio experience emphasizes again the need to actively engage school personnel in the effort. Failing to get their immediate participation because of organizational uncertainties in the central office proved detrimental to progress in the early years of San Antonio's effort. Partners reported that when the district became more involved in 2001–2002, the collaborative could move ideas along and act on them more quickly. Just as important, both the San Antonio and Santa Ana cases demonstrate the delicacy of relationships with the central office. On the one hand, using the central office as the lead in the Charlotte and Santa Ana cases resulted in adopting rather typical staff development programs that could have been funded from existing district, state, and federal coffers. On the other hand, not having the district actively engaged as in Denver and San Antonio in its early years also resulted in failing to make headway in the schools.

Collaboratives with Moderate Progress

Four other sites appeared to have developed interorganizational linkages that were fast approaching the collaboration level. However, two of them made less progress in other aspects: Jackson and Miami.

Jackson

The Jackson Public School had an enrollment of 31,800 students at the beginning of this effort. The Jackson partners had not participated in UPP and had little prior experience with collaboration. Parents for Public Schools (PPS) and others had been supported in the past by the Ford Foundation. PPS took the initiative to convene the others to discuss how to respond to the CERI RFP. The director of evaluation from the central office attended the first meeting and challenged the partners to focus on the Lanier feeder pattern, serving about 4,800 students. It not only was located in the poorest section of the district, but also was a cluster with few existing supports or initiatives. Partners agreed to this. They were

- PPS
- Mississippi Human Services Agenda
- Millsaps College
- Public Education Forum
- The Algebra Project
- Jackson Public Schools.

The district had had very high levels of turnover in superintendents during the past few years, but one initiative seemed to be remembered—a move toward site-based management that had dissolved with the turnover. The group felt that this was an essential part of engaging parents in the governance of their schools and of ensuring their interest—a major problem from their point of view. The group soon focused on site-based management as the key to school improvement and proposed that resources from the grant be used to train members of school site-management committees. In addition, to gain the buy-in from the Lanier cluster schools, the collaborative proposed to offer minigrants to the schools for their individual reform efforts. It also indicated in its proposal that it would convene principals in the cluster and offer them a specified staff development regime—called the Principals' Academy—provided by a college partner. We note that the principals were not involved in this planning stage. The Algebra Project, a major resource in Jackson to develop better math instruction, while listed as a partner, did not have a significant role to play in the initiative as described in the proposal. The proposal was approved with PPS as the lead/director. A central office

representative and other organizations were listed as equal participants on the governing board.

The 1999–2000 year of operations did not evolve as expected.
The director of the initiative, who also was director of the local PPS
chapter, seldom reconvened the members and instead acted as sole
administrator of the funds, making many decisions on her own. The
PPS lead directed the funds to largely support school grants and
modest staff development in the schools. The principals were convened and began a series of seminars run by Millsaps College.

Early interviews of partners indicated that they were not
involved in the initiative, feeling alienated by the way in which the
lead was managing the initiative. In fact, several complained of the
high-handed role of PPS. In addition, the principals, while excited
that attention was finally being paid to their cluster and enthused that
resources were coming to them, questioned the nature of their staff
development, indicating that it was not quite what they needed. They
felt that the monthly meetings that brought them together for the
first time were an important push in the right direction for progress
to be made in their schools. In interviews they expressed a newfound
sense of responsibility. In the past, they had let others tell them how
to operate and had not met as a group. By meeting as a group they
were challenged for the first time to take responsibility for their cluster. These early meetings reportedly enabled them to see the opportunity they had been handed and to take more initiative. They began
to demand more independence and requested that they be able to
determine the support they received as opposed to getting a prede-
termined set of principal professional development activities. Early
feedback from the foundation and RAND indicated that the partners
should meet and rethink their strategies.

By happenstance, the director of the Ask for More Initiative, as
it was called, moved from the area for personal reasons at the end of
the 1999–2000 school year. A new lead was chosen from outside the
existing organization to be the local director of PPS and of Ask for
More. She reviewed the different feedback available and took action.
Her first move was quite telling. According to interviews, she convened the original members and the principals as well as other organi-

zations possibly interested in CERI. At this meeting, according to participants' recollections, she "put the money on the table" and asked the principals, "How can we help you?"

After a series of meetings aided by LCN involving significant discussions around purpose, vision, and governance, a new partnership was formed. While the PPS remained the fiduciary agent and major convener, the collaborative in many respects came to be led by the Principals' Council, with the other Ask for More organizations acting as supports to the principals' efforts to improve teaching and learning within the cluster. Note, the regular Principals' Council meetings were led and organized by the principals, not by district staff. It has remained stable since the collaborative's reorganization.

The collaborative moved from giving funds away to gathering, sharing, and using data to understand key challenges. Eventually the partners and principals together with the help of the evaluation director reviewed data and identified major challenges as being poor achievement in English and math and lack of aspiration for college. They then worked together to develop activities across the cluster in concert with the schools that could address these challenges. In particular, the collaborative began using the services of the local Algebra Project provider to give staff development to teachers in the cluster. The collaborative also moved to support clusterwide decisions made by the principals. For example, beginning in 2002–2003, they supported a clusterwide "College Day." The annual college fair where students went from stall to stall was replaced by visits from counselors of nearby colleges who met with small groups of interested students throughout the day. Also, workshops that provided hands-on assistance with financial aid applications were held in the evenings for parents and students. In addition, after reorganizing itself, the collaborative helped sponsor different "school nights," aided by the district's director of evaluation, who informed parents about such matters as the new state assessment and graduation requirements. The collaborative encouraged attendance by offering refreshments and student performances.

Before the presence of Ask for More, these types of activities were unheard of in the Lanier cluster and were therefore noted by the central office. Following the lead of the Lanier cluster, the district restructured itself into smaller subdistricts administered by Principals' Councils. It also recognized the cooperative attempts of the Lanier Principals' Council and its collaborative partners and encouraged other areas to adopt some of the same approaches.

Given the slow start in Jackson, the collaborative has yet to develop a full systemic agenda, but it has moved to be able to support one. Collaborative members have joined forums and committees within the district that provide advice to the superintendent and business interests, becoming involved in these types of activities to gain stature as well as to argue for policy improvement that would serve the cluster.

Test scores at the elementary and middle school levels were found to increase across almost all schools in the cluster and all grades tested during the period that Ask for More came into being. These gains exceeded the district and state averages consistently in five of the schools. In general, test scores at Lanier High School increased slightly, while those in the district declined. High school completion rates in the Lanier cluster also increased during this period well in excess of those in the district as a whole.

While it is difficult to argue that the collaborative was responsible for all of this improvement, a prima facie case exists that the collaborative helped strengthen the improvement efforts in this cluster after an initial poor start. In particular, principals have credited the monthly meetings of the Ask for More–supported Principals' Council with enabling them to review data, identify problems and strengths, find joint solutions to common problems, and implement them in the schools.

Miami

Miami–Dade County Public Schools is one of the largest systems in the United States. It enrolled about 352,600 students at the start of this effort. The Miami site was formerly part of the UPP initiative and, like Santa Ana, had a very strong reputation within that effort. The foundation invited the following former UPP-involved organizations to respond to the proposal: the Greater Miami Urban Education Pact, University of Miami, and the Education Fund. In response, the original partners involved others. The original partners included

- Greater Miami Urban Education Pact
- Dade Public Education Fund
- Miami-Dade County Public Schools
- University of Miami, School of Education
- Billie Birnie and Associates.

Together they proposed an initiative called Central EXPRESS and focused on the Central High School feeder pattern with an enrollment of about 11,300 students. Unlike several of the other sites, it spent some time during the planning year looking at data and considering reform strategies. Members were particularly concerned about the trend of teachers leaving the cluster and thought that activities should focus on creating a collegial environment that would not only attract teachers but also enable them to fully support students using appropriate pedagogy. In addition, it was clear that students needed help on the state assessments, especially in writing. Moreover, the dropout rate was quite high and many students and parents were not fully engaged with the system. Central EXPRESS's goal was to improve student achievement, thereby increasing graduation rates as well as the ability of students to pursue desirable options after graduating. In addition, the partners developed strong relationships with principals in the cluster and with several activist parents who were eager to help improve the schools therein.

The Ford Foundation approved the grant and over the next several years five partners consistently composed the collaborative: the Urban Education Pact, the Education Fund, the University of Miami, Billie Birnie and Associates, and the Central feeder pattern schools. The Central EXPRESS steering committee consisted of the lead partners as well as other interested organizations and individuals. The lead or fiduciary agent was the Urban Education Pact. While the collaborative engaged district leaders in its work, they did not directly employ these relationships to further systemic changes across the district or even within the subdistrict.

Over the years, the partners did not further their connections to the district staff or the central office. Neither did they develop a systemic policy strand to affect district policies. Instead, they focused heavily on the development of a series of activities they thought would create a demonstration for excellent teacher, parent, and student engagement. If these activities were fully implemented and if they proved to be effective, then the partners planned to lobby for scale-up to other locations using empirical data that they collected to show effectiveness.

The plan developed by Central EXPRESS consistently focused on three areas: community engagement, student services, and professional development. Special attention was paid to nurturing collegial interactions and improving specific areas of poor student performance. These activities were not predeveloped vendor programs but relied heavily on members of the collaborative or parents and staff within the cluster to develop them. They were grounded in research and relied heavily on developing the capacity of members of the collaborative, parents, or school staff. Some of the initial activities were supported by other grants and were discontinued when the funds or program ended, such as Americorp tutoring in several cluster schools, establishment of parent resource centers, and the provision of financial support to pursue urban education and math and science masters' programs. Some programs, such as the Instructional Leadership Cadre, were dropped when the collaborative determined that they were no longer satisfactorily meeting targets' needs. When such a decision was made, the collaborative made every effort to develop new programs that could replace the old.

As in Jackson, the director of the collaborative in Miami left in 2000 for personal reasons. Unlike in Jackson, she was quickly replaced in a seamless fashion with no slowdown in collaborative functioning. The five partners made decisions via consensus and presented them at steering committee meetings for feedback and final approval. The different organizations took the lead on tasks that matched their strengths. Thus, in the actual execution of activities, each partner tended to work on its own, although partners helped one another in the development stages. Without the contributions of one another's resources and efforts, several of Central EXPRESS's activities would not have come to fruition. For example, to implement the Writing Academy, a staff development program designed to help teachers address the significant writing shortfalls of students, the Education Fund provided the public monetary match required by the Annenberg grant, and the University of Miami took charge of the activity by providing the curriculum and delivery of coursework.

Over the course of the initiative, the foundation and RAND noted the fine work being done in the cluster but pushed the partners to address the CERI goals of expansion and creation of systemic policy. Partners did not buy into these sets of activities in part because they were heavily vested in the idea of documenting empirical evidence of effectiveness and did not think that their demonstration had matured to the point where they could bring it to the district to scale up. They wanted to develop hard evidence of their works' impact prior to doing so. In addition, they argued that the size of the district was formidable and that they were too small an entity to have impact. The Ford Foundation countered that the impact could be on the subdistrict level. However, the collaborative had made few inroads there. In addition, the group did not develop plans for sustainment of the work or of the collaborative.

In spring 2002, the Ford Foundation announced plans to tie off support to Central EXPRESS. Although the structure and processes of the collaborative remained the same, loss of continued funding from the Ford Foundation created a dramatic change in the momentum and sustainability of the collaborative. The steering committee's focus with regard to collaborative work shifted from planning future activities to deciding how to scale back and complete current programs. For example, coverage for the staff member hired to carry out several of the parent and community activities was significantly reduced in the 2002–2003 school year. She was able to provide some support to community involvement specialists and the established parent resource centers, but this amount was significantly less than in previous years. Implementation declined, and policy issues and sustainment were not addressed.

As for achievement outcomes, during the CERI time period, the schools posted test-score increases on different exams. In fact eight of the eleven schools posted gains in excess of district and state gains in math, a subject specifically targeted as a problem area by the cluster. Seven of the schools posted significant gains in writing, a focus of the collaborative work. A prima facie case exists that the collaborative might have helped the schools in their efforts to improve writing scores. Cluster completion rates, however, did not improve during this period, although efforts were made to forge stronger communication among teachers, principals, and other school staff of the various cluster schools.

Reflections

While both these sites developed collaborative linkages over time, we note that at the time of our last visit in spring 2003, Jackson was moving forward, while the Miami collaborative was beginning to slip in part because of the loss of Ford Foundation funding. In contrast to the other sites discussed so far, these two made significantly more progress toward the goals set out by the foundation for the following reasons:

- Their leadership had the skills and instincts to bring members together on joint projects rather than encouraging business as usual.
- The collaboratives actively involved the principals and school personnel and parents in the process, listening to their needs and avoiding replication of existing initiatives.
- The collaboratives understood that one purpose of CERI was to make a significant difference in the quality of teaching and learning, and they focused their efforts there.

We also note that both collaboratives experienced a turnover in their leadership during 1999–2000, but this did not appear to have negative consequences. The difference between the two sites lay in their divergent views on the systemic policy aspects of the initiative. The Miami site was not comfortable with this role; the Jackson site was just beginning to explore the possibilities.

Collaboratives with Significant Progress

Cataño and D.C. offer contrasts to the other sites in terms of the extent to which they expanded their visions and to which they moved toward implementing sustainable strategies. They took different paths from each other and ended up in quite different places but still made significant progress toward the Ford Foundation's vision of collaboration supporting education reform.

Cataño

In the late 1990s, the Commonwealth of Puerto Rico passed a law decentralizing the school systems and providing for considerable site-based management of the schools, seriously weakening the power of central district offices. Prior to that time, the commonwealth had exercised, through the central offices, considerable top-down control over the schools, their curriculum and instruction, and hiring and firing of teachers and administrators. Pedagogy could be described as skill and drill with very little teacher or student creativity encouraged. With this new law came an opportunity to establish new pedagogies within the commonwealth that might encourage students to stay past the sixth grade—the exit point for a majority of them.

Cataño grantees, as in Denver, Miami, and Santa Ana, had been a UPP site. The partners in the collaborative were well aware of the situation within the commonwealth. In fact, the representatives of the organization leading the collaborative were proponents of more-progressive pedagogies, viewing them as the means by which to improve teaching and to motivate students to stay past the sixth grade. The partners saw the CERI grant as an opportunity to demonstrate the potential of new pedagogy, more collegial teacher interactions, and more autonomy of the schools. Thus Cataño successfully responded to the RFP, making it by far the smallest of the districts included in the CERI effort, with a student enrollment of about 4,800 students. The original partners included

- University of the Sacred Heart
- College Board (Puerto Rico Office)
- ASPIRA of Puerto Rico
- Puerto Rico Community Foundation
- Commonwealth of Puerto Rico Department of Education
- Cataño School District.

The planning year was spent reviewing data and developing ideas for the demonstration. Cataño partners developed a series of integrated program activities based on their review of best practices. These included interventions to build motivation of students through clubs, provide parent and family workshops, establish a Principals' Council, offer staff development activities, implement a specific curriculum intervention called "SED" (the Spanish acronym for "Seminar for the Enrichment of Teaching) that involved hands-on and reflective activities for students, offer a master's program for teachers, provide mini-internships for teachers to visit excellent schools, administer student self-assessments and skills inventories, and develop new tests. The goal of the collaborative was to develop parts to integrate into a comprehensive framework for school improvement.

Rather than directing the school staff to undertake the program, the partners offered their services to schools and helped them to assess their needs and to develop individual school plans and approaches. The general idea was to help the schools and the district learn by doing and to develop school capabilities toward improvement. Services were sometimes delivered or developed by individual groups. For example the College Board created assessments, but input was gathered from all parties and used to improve the instruments. Resources were shared among the parties in the development of the tests and several partners contributed significant time and resources toward the products. Over the four years, the activities in Cataño deepened within the schools.

The University of the Sacred Heart was the lead in this endeavor. A well-known and respected education specialist who had been part of the driving force behind the UPP was director of the CERI effort. However, he decided to retire about one year into the initiative. The university selected as new project director a protégé of the former director. The two worked together throughout 2000–2001 to ensure a smooth handoff of the project. There appeared to be no ill effects from this turnover.

The members worked to establish and maintain critical relationships with the mayor of Cataño and the Department of Education for the commonwealth, garnering interest in its programs and activities. It built the relationships that would allow it to gain support over the years to eventually expand its demonstration program to other locales. When the opportunity presented itself, the collaborative was in a position to bid on a commonwealth RFP that would enable the expansion of its ideas to other sites. In 2002–2003, the demonstration program was introduced to five new districts in Puerto Rico. The intention was to expand this to other districts if successful.

In moving forward with the demonstration program, the collaborative sought the help of LCN. With its support, the collaborative developed the plan needed to help expand the program to other sites. Cataño used commonwealth funds to do so. In addition, it applied for and received grants from the Kellogg Foundation and the Puerto Rico Department of Education to help continue its work.

From its inception, the collaborative in Cataño was also concerned with the policy implications of CERI activities. Although the new law decentralizing the school systems in the commonwealth had passed, the Puerto Rico Department of Education still prescribed detailed policies governing schools and classrooms, including professional development structures, curriculum, scheduling, and even teaching practices. The collaborative targeted several of these policies and hoped that the efforts in Cataño would demonstrate the feasibility of site-based management strategies and less top-down imposition of rules. To this end, the collaborative worked closely with representatives from the Department of Education, including representatives in the governance structures, requesting exemptions from various policies as necessary.

The collaborative was challenged in 2002–2003. Review of test score data from 2001–2002 indicated that the interventions were not having the effects intended. On the one hand, test scores were not going up as desired. On the other hand, more students were staying in school and increasing the class sizes in the middle school and early years of high school. Collaborative members met over a series of several months to discuss these results and the implications for collaborative work. These discussions were led in part by the College Board, an expert in evaluation. Cataño was one of the few collaboratives that had such a resource partner. Discussions centered on whether the nature of the interventions had to change or whether they should become more universal—touching more students. While the test results were disappointing, the activities around data-review and development of improvements were considered positive.

Specifically, regarding achievement outcomes, scores on the Pruebas Portorriquenas (achievement tests) tended to increase at the third-grade level at rates greater than the commonwealth but not at the higher grade levels where many of the curriculum and instructional interventions had been implemented. Average test scores on College Board assessments, with few exceptions, declined as did scores on a practice test for college entrance. Analysis of scores for students attending the SED classes versus those who were not failed to show clear improvements associated with attendance. Completion rates, however, told a different story. While completion rates for high school did not increase, the collaborative found that a greater number of children were remaining through the middle school and early high school grades. It is this complex picture that was brought to the attention of the collaborative by the College Board and resulted in significant review of its efforts.

District of Columbia

The District of Columbia Public Schools enrolled about 71,890 students at the beginning of this effort. The site was not part of the UPP and had little history of collaboration. In fact, the city was known for having many different community-based organizations each arguing for its particular view of education reform, ranging from better facilities to vouchers. Prior to CERI, in 1997 the Ford Foundation had provided funding to the National Coalition of Activists to convene the many community-based organizations in the District for the purpose of determining a strategy for school improvement. This effort led to the coalescence of a group of individuals dedicated to creating a more unified approach to improving the D.C. schools. The RFP was sent to members of this group and they were convened by Network for Educators on the Americas (NECA) who later became the fiscal lead.

NECA moved to involve a very large group in the planning year, including different organizations, principals, teachers, and private citizens. The planning year was spent identifying the issues in D.C., conducting research on problems, and discussing possible solutions. A two-pronged approach to reform was developed. The first was to provide professional development services and engage the community in a handful of schools in the Columbia Heights–Shaw area of the city. This was a strategy similar to several other sites' efforts. The second prong was a very deliberate development of a policy agenda.

Importantly, while individuals from the district were included in this effort, the partners did not move to include the district as a whole. Rather, they argued that the central office was seen as part of the problem. In addition, they claimed that efforts to build strong relations with a superintendent would be futile given that superintendents turned over at a rapid rate. Instead they chose to include mid-level members of the district structure who they thought would survive in the long haul and who would be the "inside" proponents for reform. The original partners included

- Network for Educators on the Americas
- American Youth Policy Forum
- Center for Artistry in Teaching
- Columbia Heights–Shaw Family Support Collaborative
- D.C. Area Writing Project
- D.C. Public Schools (DCPS)

- Education Trust
- George Mason University
- Howard University
- Institute for Educational Leadership
- Listen, Inc.
- Multicultural Community Services
- National Center for Fair and Open Testing
- Parents United
- University of the District of Columbia
- Teach for America
- Tellin' Stories
- University of Maryland
- The Urban Initiative.

Finally, the partners felt that members from all the different organizations could voice their organization's views in avenues already open to them. Thus, this was not to be what the collaborative would be about. They decided that the collaborative would best be used to develop a distinctly neutral voice that could unite the community in encouraging systemwide improvements. It proposed the creation of an organization called DC VOICE, housed under NECA but operating independently. The proposal was approved and work was begun.

The team developed and delivered professional development seminars for several schools in the cluster area—but not across the whole cluster. The schools it chose enrolled about 3,100 students. As it moved forward, it began to see that its cluster-level activities, while helpful to the schools, could not be sustained or scaled up without significant resources or changes to policies. Furthermore it saw that the main benefit to the collaborative of these activities was building its reputation as a reform-minded organization interested in helping to improve school personnel.

Thus, early on, D.C. members stated that working in the cluster schools could only be a small part of their efforts. If the collaborative was going to succeed, the members felt that they had to change the way that the central office thought about teacher quality. They also had to change the way that parents and the community participated in education. Having made this decision, a considerable part of its effort went into the development of a Districtwide strategy for improving quality teaching supports. The collaborative undertook a review of data within the central office indicating the quality of teaching; a review of national research on high-quality teaching and how to support it; and a series of focus groups with teachers and others to determine their views of what was needed to ensure high-quality teaching within the district. Over a year or so two themes became obvious. First, the DCPS was trying to put in place instructional and pedagogical models of high-quality teaching; the collaborative could do little to improve on that effort. Second, the DCPS did not have in place the infrastructure to support these models. Teachers and administrators reported failure of many systems routinely taken for granted in other locales, including textbook provision, timely payment of teacher salaries and benefits, facilities repairs, mentoring, and effective recruiting practices. The collaborative then decided that to effect change, it would focus on "support for high-quality teaching" at the District level.

By the 2000–2001 school year, the collaborative began an outreach program that included seminars, focus groups, brochures to voters, presentations to the Board of Education, etc., to publicize its findings from national research as well as its own D.C.-based research on what was needed to support high-quality teaching. The outreach also was intended to advocate for a more supportive infrastructure within DCPS. As this effort grew, the collaborative continued its school-level activities but with reduced emphasis. Although recognized as useful, these activities were never expanded to other sites.

By the end of the 2000–2001 school year, the partners also focused on sustainment. They felt that DC VOICE should become a completely independent entity. With that belief, they began to work with the Public Education Fund to develop their independence. In addition, they asked LCN to help them develop strategic plans for their work. This resulted in a very pragmatic set of benchmarks for the organization as well as a broader view about the balance among its different activities. Over the course of two years they filed papers for

501(c)(3) status and spun off from NECA. They also began developing their own board. In addition, they pursued several funding opportunities to help sustain themselves in the short term.

As for achievement outcomes, the test-score results in those schools that interacted with the collaborative do not show a clear pattern. All posted increases, but only some of these were at rates higher than the District as a whole. Completion rates in the high schools increased over time. In truth, much of the effort of the collaborative went to parental involvement activities and the push for systemic change. Thus, in this time frame, the collaborative itself did not expect test score increases to result from its efforts.

Reflections

Cataño and D.C. stood out from the other sites not only in the way they functioned as collaboratives but also in terms of their success at reaching levels of implementation not seen by the others. Importantly, Cataño had had years of experience as a collaborative while the D.C. partners did not. Nevertheless, both groups had leadership that apparently grasped the fundamentals of collaborative actions and understood the politics of the local area. In addition, both focused on the development of activities that could lead to improved teaching and learning—albeit taking very different paths. Both used the services of LCN to further their efforts and move toward self-sustainment. Each saw CERI not as a way to uphold the status quo but as the way to pursue new opportunities to effect change.

Discussion

Our findings lend support to the proposition in the literature that collaborative formation is a challenge in and of itself and that one should expect such advanced interorganizational linkages to develop slowly and perhaps unevenly. We saw examples of partnerships that failed to develop, implying that this approach to reform is not certain. However, our data indicated that several did grow and progress toward both their stated goals and those of the sponsor.

Sites developed different levels of interorganizational linkages, including networks, cooperation and coordination, and collaboration. All of the grantees developed networks to share information and to act cooperatively with each other. Four of the eight grantees, those in Cataño, D.C., Jackson, and Miami, made comparatively stronger progress toward the formation of deeper organizational linkages described in the literature as collaborative. Characteristics of the linkages included strong information-sharing among partners, shared or common goals, routine collection and use of data for planning and tracking progress, collaborative decisionmaking, resource pooling, joint actions or programs, clear membership rationale; active involvement of school staff and parents; and stability of members. Table 4.2 summarizes our findings concerning each collaborative with regard to these factors. The Santa Ana grantee built on a functioning partnership to bring additional grant money into the area and dedicated it to the superintendent's reform initiative. San Antonio tended primarily to coordinate the delivery of each member's preexisting activities to the target cluster. Grantees in Denver and Charlotte made weaker progress in the development of organizational linkages. While they maintained network linkages, they struggled to build shared goals and to create joint operations or products through spring 2003.

At least some part of the explanation of why progress was different among the sites involved sites' purposes in developing collaboratives or attempting to do so. Several, perhaps most, initially treated the CERI effort no differently from traditional grant-making programs. Therefore, their members never expected to make the work go further than extended networks. It took effort on the part of the foundation and its consultants to communicate the greater level of activity sought. Several sites possibly would have benefited if, in the planning year, clearer communication of the policy goals and better support by the consultants had existed.

We note that across the board, the sites struggled to gain access to, understand, and use data in constructive ways. In addition, they struggled as a group to develop strategic plans and benchmarks. Again, earlier interventions and provision of technical assistance on this front might have proved useful. However, the collaboratives themselves did not always have members who were expert in these areas. Their formation did not focus on this expertise as a necessary ingredient toward progress. Thus, it might be that better information at the initiative's beginning on what types of expertise would prove useful could have produced stronger progress.

Other factors pointed out in the literature as important sometimes had influence; in other cases they did not. For example:

- Size of the cluster or district seemed to be loosely associated with progress, although exactly how was not clear. Three of the largest sites—Miami, Charlotte, Denver—did not make as much progress as the smaller sites—Cataño and Jackson. D.C., a larger site, made significant progress.
- The number of partners in the collaborative also did not seem to be a defining factor. D.C. had by far the largest group to deal with and was quite successful in developing its efforts. Other sites, such as Denver and San Antonio, with smaller numbers of partners, either struggled to find common ground or did not create joint activities.
- Of the four sites that became collaboratives, three (Miami, D.C., and Cataño) had prior relationships among the partners—whether through UPP or other types of convenings. In contrast, prior relationships in Denver and Santa Ana did not ensure progress. With the right leader, however—as in Jackson, for example—we found that collaborative relationships could be built within the timeframe of this study. Thus, it appears that it is not so much whether prior relationships existed, but rather the nature of those relationships that was important. Also key was a mutually agreed on common cause that bound partners together. In the case of Denver, San Antonio, and Santa Ana, the prospect of new funds was a major part of what bound the members together. This proved not to be effective without other catalysts.

Table 4.2
Progress Made by the Sites Along Various Indicators Measuring Interorganizational Linkages

Interorganizational Linkages	Charlotte	Denver	San Antonio	Santa Ana
Information sharing	Yes	Yes	Yes	Yes
Shared goals	Members not strongly committed	Members not strongly committed	Less commitment over time	Yes, strongly shared
Use of data for initial problem identification	Weak	Weak	Modest	Modest
Effective collaborative decision-making	Initially top-down district-led decision-making	Lack of clear governance or decision-making authority	Networking evident, but few collaborative decisions made	Moderate, strong district-led influence
Resource pooling	Resources pooled	Resources dispersed as grants	Split into four equal shares; dispersed for existing activities	Resources pooled
Joint actions	Few actions acted on as planned over the years	No	Coordinated	Coordinated
Member rationale clear, with important constituencies represented	Members changed with shift in leadership	Members changed with reorganizations	Member rationale clear	Member rationale clear
Active inclusion of school staff and parents	Low involvement of school staff and parents	Low involvement of school staff and parents	Low involvement of school staff and parents	Strong principal council; low involvement of school staff; progress in involvement of parents
Stability of members	Changed with development of more focused vision	Changed yearly with reorganizations	Members changed in last two years	Members changed in last year

Table 4.2—continued

Interorganizational Linkages	Jackson	Miami	Cataño	D.C.
Information sharing	Yes	Yes	Yes	Yes
Shared goals	Initially weak, now building	Yes, strongly shared from beginning	Strongly shared from beginning	Building over time
Use of data for initial problem identification	Weak	Strong	Modest	Modest, encumbered by poor district data
Effective collaborative decision-making	After first year, strong collaborative decisionmaking	Strong collaborative decisionmaking	Strong collaborative decision-making	Strong collaborative decisionmaking
Resource pooling	Resources partially pooled; partially dispersed as mini-grants	Resources pooled	Resources pooled	Resources pooled
Joint actions	Yes	Yes	Yes	Yes
Member rationale clear, with important constituencies represented	Member rationale became clear in second year	Member rationale clear, representative	Member rationale clear, representative	Member rationale clear, broad membership
Active inclusion of school staff and parents	Strong principal council; progress in parental involvement	Strong involvement in activities and governance	Strong involvement through activities, not governance	Strong involvement in activities and governance
Stability of members	Members changed in first year, then stabilized	Stable	Stable	Stable

The ability of the site leadership to bring members together in a collaborative fashion proved important to success. Collaboratives led by central office representatives proved to be less conducive to the integration of members than other forms of leadership. Among sites led by central offices (Charlotte and Santa Ana), we found that partners tended to adopt cluster activities that resembled those that the district would have been likely to adopt otherwise (i.e., that were adopted by districts across the country in response to standards-based accountability reforms). Moreover, they did not address systemic issues. However, not involving or pursuing the participation of the district at all led to problems as well, especially in the formulation of systemic initiatives, as revealed through the experiences of Denver, Miami, and San Antonio in its early years. Sites that made more progress chose a more difficult balance. The district was deemed an equal partner but one that constantly needed attention and nurturing.

Top-down management styles by leadership also were shown to be counterproductive. We saw several clear examples of the opposite, wherein more-inclusive styles of leading effectively brought members to the table and helped sustain the common vision. Sites with such leadership, namely Jackson, Cataño, D.C., and Miami, encouraged input from and collaboration with school personnel well beyond that exhibited by the other sites. They saw school personnel as being important partners in the effort. The same could be said of their relationships with parents. At these sites, members of the community were treated with respect and their opinions were sought in the development and implementation of the activities.

Our review of the data to date indicates that several other factors besides inclusive leadership were important in ensuring progress. Sites making significant progress (Cataño, Jackson, D.C.) shared three other characteristics, generally not found among the other sites. These characteristics fall under the broad headings of will and capacity:

- The most advanced sites benefited at key points from the services of an outside party with strategy expertise that helped the partners develop a broader view of the initiative, create specific plans and benchmarks, and move beyond specific impasses. They were not afraid to seek help when needed and used external providers to help build needed capability.

- They truly saw CERI as an important opportunity at a specific juncture in time that would enable the development of a new force in the community. Leaders clearly moved away from a typical grant-writing mode to fund existing activities, working toward new constructs for the community.

- They were adept at using data to understand what was taking place in their communities and in moving the initiative forward. D.C. and Cataño in particular had strong research or evaluative partners, while Jackson was developing this expertise with the help of the district evaluation director. This expertise was also available in Miami.

CHAPTER FIVE

Themes from CERI

The initial results of CERI, as outlined in the preceding chapter, indicated that there is potential for collaboratives to be created and sustained in local communities. This statement is based on our assessment that four of the eight sites successfully formed functioning collaboratives and that three of these four made progress toward institutionalizing their respective reform efforts. Overall, the actual and potential impact varied greatly across all eight sites. Although the scope and duration of this study precludes assertions with regard to "successful strategies" for forming and sustaining collaboratives, the analysis does point to a number of themes that emerged across sites.

There is little evidence to suggest that these tentative lessons apply to other sites, but they do represent a pattern of findings about "what matters" that potentially could be instructive to future efforts intended to create and sustain collaboratives. These themes should also be useful to funders that support such efforts and to the eight sites as they continue to grow and develop.

This chapter presents themes regarding factors that seemed important in describing progress of the CERI sites. They are based on reflections of collaborative members and patterns that emerged from the qualitative data.

Networking Was an Important First Step and a Challenge by Itself

Of the eight funded sites, all developed interorganizational linkages that promoted the sharing of information among partners. Interviews revealed that members at each site believed that the efforts sponsored by the CERI grant led to stronger networks in the community than had previously existed. Moreover, the efforts resulted in a greater propensity to work together in cooperative ways, both during the life of the grant and into the future.

In this regard, the CERI experience was deemed as successful across all sites. In fact, interviews of collaborative members often focused on how the members had "talked together" for the first time about important educational issues. Members often emphasized that these conversations were huge first steps in their communities. When queried about whether they had made progress past this talking stage, several commented in approximately the same way, "You don't understand how difficult it has been just to talk. We never even did that before. It will take time to build trust to work together." The experiences echoed the literature, which indicates that just sitting down around the table together and building trust levels is a slow process.

Collaborative members also noted the difficulty of even accomplishing something as simple as meeting face to face. Obviously, it was difficult just to schedule meetings at times convenient for all. Solutions to the meeting challenge were straightforward:

- Commit to meet at regular times on a regular basis—for example, the first Monday of the month at a specific time and place.
- Work around the time of the most difficult people to schedule. Oftentimes this proved to be the school principals who were loath to leave their schools during hours when students were on campus. In Jackson, where the principals became a core part of the collaborative, meetings eventually moved to a time most convenient for them, guaranteeing their attendance.

- Create a Web-based communications network. While this worked well in D.C., where the collaborative put significant resources into its development, it worked less well in San Antonio where the Web-based system was not well developed to distinguish important meeting messages from a larger flow of mail traffic.

Decisionmaking was often stalled when collaboratives did not use these scheduling and communication techniques or were slow in developing them. Moreover, less was accomplished when members did not make meetings or sent "seconds" in their place.

Stakeholder Involvement Was Necessary

To determine which stakeholders the collaborative should include, or perhaps more important, were necessary not to exclude, collaboratives assessed the "lay of the land," seeking organizations that held power and influence in education. The types of organizations that held power and influence varied across sites and included such entities as local foundations, teachers' unions, advocacy groups, and government agencies, to name a few. Some sites identified key individuals who exercised influence as consultants or advisors to the school district. Sites also often recruited organizations with particular expertise as they defined and focused their goals and activities. For example, when Santa Ana began focusing more on public engagement, it reached out to local community involvement organizations. Sites also benefited from involving such school-level people as teachers and principals. Involving the front-line implementers enhanced the chances of collaborative activities being not only relevant but also implemented.

The membership varied across sites, and no patterns emerged to suggest a particular size or number of members was ideal. However, broad membership across critical stakeholder groups was key to establishing the collaboratives' legitimacy in several cases because it signaled impartiality among prospective local stakeholders. For example, the value of broad-based membership was particularly apparent in D.C., where policymakers and the general public were skeptical of community organizations that represented a particular constituency group (e.g., parents) or policy approach (e.g., vouchers).

Finally, organizations only made sense as partners if they were willing to work jointly. For example, the Miami collaborative initially sought involvement from the influential business community but ultimately abandoned its recruitment efforts when the businesses expressed little initiative or interest in participating in the collaborative. Likewise, the D.C. collaborative broke ties early with an organization that expressed interest in jointly pursuing funding but little interest in working collaboratively. The two collaboratives argued that the costs of pursuing these relationships, in terms of expended energy, would not have been justified by the potential gains.

Effectively Involving School Staff Supported Progress

The literature review indicated very little about the ideal composition of collaboratives, other than that membership should be determined by the goals or vision of the collaborative and that major stakeholders in those goals should be included. However, the implementation literature is very clear about the importance of involving school staff in planning and development. The foundation's vision for CERI supported this construct. Given that its initiative was to involve a set of activities to be implemented at the school-cluster level, the foundation encouraged active involvement of school staff and parents in collaboratives, seeing this as a strategy by which to engage in achieving high-quality teaching and learning in a specific cluster of schools.

Initially, few sites had prominent roles for these two groups. Charlotte, Denver, and San Antonio never developed strong relations with the schools, and this in part led to their lack of progress. In Charlotte, the principals in particular were unable or unwilling to involve themselves in the effort, leading to lack of implementation in the schools. Denver included school staff—primarily principals—as active members of the collaborative's governing structure. However, in Denver the principals as well as other members could never quite figure out what their role was or, for that matter, what the collaborative's purpose was. In San Antonio, the school staff were not heavily involved in part because of the turnover of the principals.

Grantees in D.C. and in Jackson offered a different approach. The Jackson Principals' Council was especially effective in pushing the collaborative forward. In contrast, D.C. principals and teachers were active members of the steering committee and other parts of the governance structure from the very beginning. In both D.C. and Jackson, groups representing parents were major partners in the initial collaborative organization and continued to be throughout. The purpose of parent inclusion was to see them more heavily involved in the support of education reform efforts. In addition, both groups involved school staff.

Other grantees involved parents but usually not as part of the formal structure, at least initially. For example, Miami and San Antonio adopted activities to increase parental involvement but did not include parents or parent organizations in the governing structure of the collaborative. While Santa Ana included in its proposal the Parent Advisory Council as a member of its collaborative's governing structure, in reality it had more of a marginal advisory role.

Cataño had a unique three-tier governance structure that effectively involved parents and school staff. The Executive Committee consisted of the directors of each partner and met only once or twice a year. The Program Committee consisted of the field representatives and staff who implemented CERI activities and plans on a broad level and met once a month. The District Planning Committee also met once a month and made the detailed decisions about which activities should be carried out. Parents, teachers, support staff, and all principals participated in decisionmaking at this level, and no activities were carried out without approval by this inclusive group.

Leads' Legitimacy Strengthened Collaborative Formation

We found that the ability to pull together a collaborative was closely associated with the perceived legitimacy and authority of the lead organization. Several examples provided insights into the tensions involved in the leadership role during the early stages of collaborative formation.

At all sites, the school district was logically a critical stakeholder whose involvement was considered necessary to expedite desirable changes. In fact, as discussed in Chapter Four, the school district was the initial lead of the collaborative in two sites (Santa Ana and Charlotte). As a result, the CERI efforts in these two sites were perceived as initiatives or programs of the districts. This perception, coupled with the district's authority over schools, resulted in fast adoption of professional development and other school-based activities. However, the initial activities in Santa Ana and Charlotte tended to resemble typical district efforts and not the systemic reform that the Ford Foundation intended collaboratives to create. For example, Santa Ana used CERI funds to purchase professional development and curriculum materials, such as Move-It-Math and Read Plus, programs typically purchased by school districts with Title I funding. These efforts in Santa Ana, as in many other districts, focused on improving traditional in-servicing and classroom-level practice of individual teachers without changing school structures or policies that posed systemic barriers to the improvement of practice.

In these two sites, community members and school personnel often thought that the lead organization possessed significant authority but lacked legitimacy because it had no objective perspective. The central office was often seen as part of the problem. Therefore, it could not lead members to the solution.

After the first year of CERI, the Ford Foundation voiced its concern that Santa Ana and Charlotte were pursuing traditional district efforts rather than system reform, and both collaboratives ultimately decided to shift fiduciary responsibilities out of the district. In Charlotte, this shift in funding authority coincided with a substantive shift in focus, but it is unclear whether the two shifts were related. Charlotte did, however, begin to focus on systemic issues of recruiting and retaining teachers and school leaders. The district's relinquishment of formal control of funding might or might not have had real implications for the collaborative's funding decisions, but the shift symbolically assisted the site in representing its collaborative as community efforts rather than district initiatives.

This is not to suggest that central offices should not be included in collaboratives. In general, sites learned that district involvement was crucial but that the district was not necessarily an appropriate lead for a collaborative effort aimed at systemic change. Several sites recognized that community organizations needed to be on the outside pressuring for change but also have influence inside the central office to gain access to schools and teachers. This proved to be a crucial balancing act for several collaboratives. For example, because the Puerto Rico Department of Education was highly politicized and much decisionmaking was influenced by party affiliation, Cataño had to carefully balance its contacts and influence with each elected administration. Relationships established with one administration could be destroyed when the next administration came into office. When a change in governing parties did in fact occur, the collaborative rode it out without undue loss of progress, in part because it kept its reputation as being an outside group friendly to all parties interested in improving schools.

In contrast to Charlotte and Santa Ana, DC VOICE recognized that the initiative would be dead in the water if led by the central office. Suspicions of the existing bureaucracy ran high in the community. It was essential for the collaborative to be seen as legitimately serving the needs of the community. Whether by foresight or by happenstance, the collaborative developed a leadership team composed of people with strong standing among the different community factions, including a former school board member known for "reaching out and including people" and for her expertise in school issues. It developed a governing structure of a small steering committee made up of parties known for their leadership in improving the schools; a set of action committees with membership appropriate to the tasks at hand; and a broader-based set of organizations that met less often but provided strong input into what DC VOICE should become when together.

In D.C., the collaborative rejected having the superintendent directly involved. In their view, the superintendent was likely to turn over too soon, so his or her commitment would not have meaning in the long term. Instead, DC VOICE focused on ensuring the involvement of high-ranking members of the permanent central office staff known to them from other venues. In their view, this involvement was at the right level to add authority and insight. The collaborative then chose to influence elected officials in other ways. A D.C. collaborative member explained, "It's a two way street. We need the super's blessing before going into schools. Simultaneously, we are working with [D.C.] council members to ask hard questions of the school system [and the superintendent]." Through this balance of legitimacy, objectivity, and broad-based inclusion, DC VOICE became within a few years a recognized player in the District and known for its objective information on teacher quality supports. At the same time, D.C. members explained that involving the District was not just about gaining access to the schools or to data but gaining access to the system itself. Collaboratives needed entrée into their district to enable conversations with district leaders regarding systemic change in district structures and policies.

Much of the story behind the Denver collaborative's failure to thrive can be traced to initial leadership that lacked legitimacy or authority. As explained in the previous chapters, the early development of the collaborative was tossed back and forth between the community-based organizations and the superintendent's office with no clear steps toward finding a strong legitimate leader who could draw the parties together. When finally funded, the leadership was given to a relatively unknown member of the lead organization who lacked the legitimacy or authority among the parties, especially the schools, to pull the disparate groups together.

The Manner of How Collaborative Members Worked Together Determined Growth

As described in Chapter Two, collaboration is the strongest form of interorganizational linkage. It is defined by common goals, joint work, and shared products. Despite broad-based membership of influential stakeholders, we found some efforts falling short of collaboration (i.e., their work could be characterized as networking, cooperation, or coordination). The member organizations in San Antonio, for example, worked cooperatively to implement their respective programs. The work by and large was not new. It was a continuation of existing activities that were carried out separately by the member organizations. While CERI might have resulted in better coordination of the existing activities, it did not yield synergy. By pursuing "business as usual," San Antonio failed to engage in activities that could have led to fundamental shifts in the education system.

D.C.'s membership, on the other hand, consisted primarily of individuals with only moderate clout acting alone but with a great deal of influence as a collective and collaborative group. The D.C. collaborative not only engaged in new activities, it created an entirely new organization known as DC VOICE. In doing so, the collaborative members formalized and institutionalized their commitment to a common mission. The members of the collaborative worked very much as a team, and it was often difficult to trace attribution of an activity to any one particular member. Much of the collaborative's work was jointly planned by the collaborative members and carried out by DC VOICE's staff. By coming together and promoting a comprehensive and common vision of systemic reform, the collaborative members were able to further their own work as well as the goals of DC VOICE itself.

Leadership Style Played a Role in Collaborative Development

Several sites benefited from strong leaders throughout various stages of their collaborative's development. Leaders needed to be able to build trusting relationships, effectively communicate the collaborative's goals and vision, motivate collaborative members to act, and encourage reflection and improvement of strategies. Initially, collaborative leaders had to have clear ideas about how to mobilize a collaborative effort, including who to involve and how to facilitate consensus-building among disparate groups who in many cases had never worked together before.

The story of the Jackson collaborative's revival, inspired by a leadership change, best illustrated the importance of leadership style. As discussed in Chapter Four, the collaborative was initially led in a heavy-handed way. The original leadership of the collaborative, as well as the strategies employed to bring different organizations together, tended to alienate the members. Groups that had agreed to take part in the CERI work with the lead organization, PPS, reported not being heavily involved in the writing of the grant proposal or the strategic planning of activities to be carried out. In fact, few of the organizations knew what substantive roles they could play in this endeavor. PPS, as fiscal lead, became the de facto primary decision-maker. The change in leadership that occurred in late 2000 not only brought about stronger participation by other collaborative members but also gave principals more significant control of the initiative. The new leadership transformed PPS's role into that of "lead convener," and exerted a more inclusive style of involving others, thereby initiating true collaborative decisionmaking and joint work.

All collaborative members reported that collaboration involved long and hard work, and therefore required leadership capable of motivating members to push through the difficult times. As one Miami collaborative member put it, "Collaborative work takes more effort. Trying to get six people going in the same direction as opposed to just one person is more difficult. The gain can be greater if it works, but it takes a good leader to make it happen." In Miami, the leadership held retreats to celebrate progress and motivate people to strive for the long-term goals. These meetings built a sense of solidarity and hope, despite the challenges the collaborative faced.

In addition to pushing partners forward, effective leaders encouraged collaborative members to stand back and reflect on the degree to which their efforts were meeting the needs of the targeted community. They then led a process of revision if necessary. Leaders also encouraged membership to think about the future, including whether certain activities should be continued and if so, how. For example, leaders in Santa Ana used test scores and school feedback to assess the success of activities it was pursuing and made decisions accordingly.

Building the Legitimacy of the Collaborative Proved Critical for Sustainment

Although leaders with legitimacy in the community could help propel collaboratives, in the long term collaboratives themselves had to gain legitimacy as voices for educational improvement. Legitimacy was important in obtaining buy-in from key stakeholders, particularly school-level people and parents. These groups faced competing demands for their time, and were only willing to participate in—or even cooperate with—collaboratives when they perceived them to be genuine and worthwhile. Legitimacy also proved critical to site progress because it provided collaboratives with clout and the access necessary to influence policymakers. In some cases, collaborative members included high-ranking district personnel who were in a position to alter policy, but, in most cases, collaboratives had to have legitimacy to gain access to policymakers. Many different factors contributed to a collaborative's perceived legitimacy, including the reputation of collaborative leaders and/or partner organizations, the perceived objectivity of the collaborative's approach, the relevance of collaborative goals and activities to local needs, and the ability to make a contribution to the solution of the problem at hand.

Well-known and respected leaders lent credibility and legitimacy to collaboratives. As one respondent put it, "To leverage change, power players need to be part of the collaborative." Although powerful leaders greatly increased the influence of their respective collaboratives, it was problematic when collaboratives' legitimacy was derived solely from leadership and not the larger membership. This was initially a problem in Charlotte where the collaborative started as a project of the district and was therefore not seen as something new or separate. The collaborative was able to influence teachers and principals but only because of the district's authority. When the collaborative realized that the district's role needed to be deemphasized, the collaborative had to find new sources of legitimacy.

To the extent that collaboratives grounded their work in data and research, stakeholders respected their objectivity. D.C., for example, possessed a great deal of legitimacy because it was seen as an unbiased community organization in a city full of advocacy groups. One policymaker explained, "Right now, when the mayor thinks about teacher quality, he calls DC VOICE. There is no one else to call . . . they are the only game in town." D.C. and other sites gained this reputation in part because they consisted of broad-based membership that included, but was not dominated by, the school district; reviewed the research and articulated it clearly for local policymakers too busy to attend to it; listened to the needs of the local community, including parents, teachers, principals, and students through focus groups, speakers' series, and everyday contact; and kept asking "How can we help make the schools better?" rather than promoting a specific solution from the start.

Related to objectivity, collaboratives were respected when they were perceived as "on target" or "in tune with the real issues." The collaboratives that listened to the perspectives of multiple stakeholders were able to identify areas of consensus in the community regarding problems that needed to be addressed. In an indirect way, the Ford Foundation's emphasis on working with a cluster of schools brought legitimacy and credibility to the collaboratives. It was their roles in individual schools speaking with individual teachers, students, and parents that cemented the reputations of collaborative members as experts who could help. This was true in Cataño, D.C., Jackson, and Miami where the cluster-level programs allowed them to establish their credentials and brought them firsthand knowledge of conditions in schools.

Finally, the legitimacy of collaboratives depended on the degree to which they were perceived as contributing to the schools in the community that they attempted to influence. Cataño, D.C., Jackson, Miami, San Antonio, and Santa Ana each were widely credited with specific progress in schools and, in some cases, credited with improvements in student achievement. For example, many people gave the Miami collaborative credit for increased writing scores in their cluster. As a result, it became well known and respected by many school and district personnel. Accomplishing results also served an internal purpose of building trust and motivation among collaborative members.

Adeptly Using Information Helped Identify Key Issues

In our initial sets of interviews with collaborative members across sites, we found that despite their having a full planning year prior to the proposal, few had gained access to enough data to understand what issues plagued schools. Most were familiar with test-score data and state-reported dropout rates but not much more. It appeared that the sites had largely used the planning year to develop collaboratives or to cement collaborative relationships in those already functioning.

Collaboratives provided different reasons for lack of data analysis. First, as already indicated, collaborative interactions proved to be difficult and important to establish. Second, if the collaborative did not have members inside the central office, it was difficult for them to gain access to data. Third, even when collaboratives had this membership, sometimes central offices did not know what information to look at. Finally, limited funding in the planning year did not allow the actors to request, develop, or analyze data. Rather, discussions were often based on the expertise already at the table and data easily available from newspaper accounts or from inside member's heads. For the most part, collaboratives did not seek members with expertise in data analysis, resulting in the absence of this skill at the table. Searches for new approaches to problems were often forestalled in the same manner. Despite the full planning year, collaboratives did not always look for new and different means of solving problems.

The Ford Foundation, in turn, did not require grantees to report in any detail base-level information and subsequent changes in quantitative outcomes. Sites were asked to include data in annual reports of activities, but without specific instructions, the writeups were very general and lacked even basic levels of data and analysis.

Our study found that the goals and activities developed by sites were more appropriate and effective when collaboratives used data to assess their local contexts, gathered research to identify appropriate strategies, and made explicit connections describing how their chosen activities would lead to their goals.

Several sites, including Cataño, D.C., Jackson, and Miami, used these strategies to craft their visions. Without ignoring the Ford Foundation's areas of focus, each site critically examined their unique situations and thoughtfully crafted visions that reflected the needs of their communities. They did not conduct this process overnight but took time to look at data and consult numerous stakeholders. In some cases, people who had already done this type of research were founding members of the collaborative. This process of assessing the local context allowed them to develop visions that rose above the headline issues and reflected the underlying problems facing their communities. D.C., for example, conducted focus groups of teachers, parents, and students to understand their perceptions of the supports needed for high-quality teaching and learning to take place and to learn where those supports were lacking. In this way, D.C. not only gathered data to diagnose the problems but also measured the extent to which resources were or were not currently available to address them.

Not all collaborative members had a clear and accurate understanding of their site's issues, strengths, and challenges. As a result, sites sometimes misdiagnosed or failed to capture the full nature of the problem, often because they failed to study available data and make a clear connection between the problems faced by schools and the activities they were proposing. For example, Denver articulated a broad goal of transforming its cluster into a demonstration site of exemplary urban education and decided to target principal leadership and on-site coaching of teachers as two of six strategies aimed at reaching the goal. However, it did not collect information that would have shown it that this strategy duplicated efforts that were under way.

RAND played a role in providing data about local context to sites in early stages. The first-year reports included data regarding site demographics and stakeholder views of the economic and political climate, educational issues, and community. In addition, the reports included summaries of a RAND survey of teacher attitudes about professional development, K–12 alignment, and public engagement. Many sites reported that this data provided new and interesting information. For example, many were surprised to learn that most teachers felt that they were already reaching out to parents but that their efforts were yielding limited results.

In addition to using data to understand the local context, sites also benefited from using research to identify and adapt activities rather than build new ideas from scratch. In Miami, for example, one collaborative member was knowledgeable about current research in effective teacher professional development and was able to encourage the collaborative to embed research-based practices into the professional development activities that it was developing and providing to teachers.

Regular Data Analysis and Reflection Enabled Beneficial Adaptation

The Ford Foundation's emphasis on demonstrating impact on outcomes indirectly emphasized continuity of collaborative activities. However, given that the initial stages of any policy or program are likely to result in incomplete implementation caused by unforeseen constraints, collaboratives that regularly reviewed data were effective in assessing what was or was not working and why and then making adjustments accordingly. For example, after two years of conducting a highly regarded Instructional Leadership Cadre, Miami realized that attendance was decreasing and therefore decided to pursue a different structure and format for working with teacher leaders. Availability of data, such as attendance and feedback forms, facilitated these reflective conversations. In the case of some sites, the data reinforced the current mode of operation. As mentioned earlier, leadership played a critical role in encouraging and facilitating a reflective, data-driven adjustment process.

Data used for reflection and improvement could be quantitative or qualitative in nature. In addition to reviewing traditional indicators, such as student achievement results and attendance, some collaboratives systematically collected qualitative data through focus groups, surveys, and feedback forms. After its restructuring, the Charlotte collaborative, for example, began surveying departing teachers to gather information that could inform its teacher-retention efforts. D.C.'s use of feedback forms at collaborative events was another example of systematic attempts to collect information for the purpose of informing the collaborative of "what was working" and "what was not," thereby enabling it to improve.

The Cataño collaborative may offer the clearest example of the use of data to improve. In their fourth year of work, it became clear from test-score results that the collaborative's interventions were not working as planned. The College Board partners brought this to the attention of partners, and a very difficult review of programs ensued. It is not known yet whether proposed improvements will result in higher test scores, but nonetheless, the point is that the collaborative attempted to use data systematically to ensure improvement over time.

Planning for Sustaining the Collaborative and Scaling Up the Reform Agenda Needed to Be Addressed Early

As we reported in Chapter Four, most sites struggled with sustainment. They remained heavily dependent on the Ford Foundation for their survival despite self-articulated beliefs that their collaborative should be sustained. The exceptions were Cataño, D.C., and Santa Ana. Each was able to procure significant funding in addition to the CERI grant. These sites were more successful because they began thinking about possible alternative sources of funding early in their development and invested time and effort to seeking other grants.

Attempts to sustain the collaborative's reform agenda in Cataño, D.C., and Santa Ana were tightly coupled with their efforts to scale up. Cataño, for example, articulated two scale-up strategies. The first was a strategy whereby changes implemented in Cataño became a part of day-to-day operations in Cataño and the district became "self-sufficient." The district's ability to take ownership of the reform agenda was enabled by the collaborative's efforts to build capacity within the district using a "train the trainers" model. As part of this model, teachers, principals, and parents who emerged as key leaders in the Cataño schools helped coordinate activities in five new school districts. The second was a strategy whereby the model developed in Cataño, the "demonstration district," was in time institutionalized through the Department of Education and implemented islandwide.

The collaboratives that waited to address the issue of sustainment were too late to show any impact. Because grant-writing, building sustainable funds, and developing sustainable relationships all take time, they must be attended to from the outset. Some sites felt that they had been misled by the Ford Foundation because they originally understood, despite statements by foundation staff to the contrary, that their grants would be renewed for 10 years. When Ford later clarified, once again, that continued funding was contingent on demonstrated progress, several sites had to scramble to address issues of impact and sustainability.

In some cases, the technical assistance provider, LCN, played a constructive role in developing plans for institutionalization. Some collaborative members admitted that they had little experience or were not inclined to think about how to institutionalize their work. As a result, they found it very helpful to have support from LCN to prompt and facilitate their thinking about sustainment and scale-up. In the words of one respondent explaining the benefit of working with the technical assistance provider, "He opened my eyes to the whole business of 'scaling up' not just in terms of replicability. He also helped me to think about how to nurture the conditions in a community that would allow change and growth to happen." LCN's support was particularly critical for D.C. and Jackson as described in Chapter Four. Not all collaboratives, however, made use of the technical assistance provider. Some were unsure of how to engage LCN, while others did not feel that they needed external support. They were therefore grateful that the Ford Foundation had presented the possibility of technical assistance as a supportive option rather than as a requirement.

Strategies for sustainment and scale-up require data collection and analysis. Because all of the collaboratives began their work focused on a cluster of schools, many chose replication as their scale-up strategy. As described in the Cataño example above, the replication strategy entailed "demonstrating" or "trying out" a reform strategy in the target schools. If and when a strategy demonstrated success, the collaboratives would then approach the school district (or appropriate policymaking body) to lobby for the policy changes needed to support the reform strategy districtwide. In some cases, collaboratives found that their interventions resulted in little improvement and therefore little evidence existed to support their widespread use. This was often the case with parental involvement activities. Several collaboratives hosted events to increase parental involvement but were disappointed with the attendance and impact achieved.

In other cases, however, collaboratives believed that their activities warranted replication but failed to collect the data necessary to convince policymakers of the activities' value. For example, Miami believed that its Americorp tutoring program was worthy of continuation beyond the duration of the grant and of replication to other schools that did not have tutors. Since Miami's plans for scale-up were developed several years after initiation of the tutoring program, Miami was unable to retrospectively access the data it needed to make its case for continuation and replication of the program.

Plans for institutionalization should address systemic barriers. Recall that Ford chose to fund collaboratives because it believed they had the potential to engage in activities that could lead to fundamental shifts in the education system. This theory was based on a belief, supported by research, that systemic barriers to instructional improvement are institutionalized within school districts and that external pressure is necessary to instigate reform. To fulfill this function, it was not enough for collaboratives to implement and replicate effective activities—collaboratives also needed to affect the policy environment that prevented their widespread institutionalization. For example, by use of its Writing Academy, Miami was perhaps the most effective collaborative in raising student test scores. This innovative form of teacher professional development, however, was implemented in an artificial environment—during the summer and after school—thereby evading rather than addressing district policies that prevented all teachers within the district from participating in a Writing Academy format of professional development. Despite Miami's ability to improve student achievement, its efforts to sustain and scale up the Writing Academy failed to address the Ford Foundation's goal of alleviating systemic barriers to improved teaching and learning.

Summary

This chapter described themes that emerged from the analysis and that appeared to explain patterns of progress or lack thereof. Taken as a whole, these lessons imply that collaboratives should be attentive to issues of broad-based membership, leadership, and legitimacy. In addition, collaboratives must develop the capability to use data effectively in their planning. No evidence suggests that these lessons can be generalized to other collaborative efforts, but they do represent issues that other funders or collaborators might want to consider as they undertake similar reforms.

CHAPTER SIX
Conclusions and Observations

The purpose of our analysis was to answer three broad questions as best we could, given the limited data available from an eight-site, four-year effort. These questions were:

- Did sites show progress toward desired outcomes? If not, why not? If so, why? What other effects occurred?
- Could lessons learned or promising practices be discerned from the experiences of individual collaboratives or the group as a whole?
- Could collaboratives be effectively created by an outside influence, such as the Ford Foundation, to sustain education improvement efforts?

The following paragraphs provide the answers thus far based on observations from the Ford Foundation's CERI efforts.

Conclusions

In answer to question one, we found that the sites made different progress across the five dimensions but that overall the CERI effort to date resulted in several functioning collaboratives.

- *Dimension 1: level of development of interorganizational linkages.* All of the grantees developed networks to share information and to act cooperatively with each other. Four of the eight grantees, those in Cataño, D.C., Jackson, and Miami, made comparatively strong progress toward the formation of deeper organizational linkages as defined in the literature on collaboratives. San Antonio had difficulty operating jointly and producing joint products, functioning cooperatively instead. The Santa Ana grantee created a well-functioning partnership to bring grant money into the area. Grantees in Denver and Charlotte made weaker progress in the development of organizational linkages.

- *Dimension 2: level of development and implementation of plans for achieving high-quality teaching and learning in the cluster.* Although never fully implementing all of their activities, four grantees contributed to the development and implementation of high-quality teaching and supports in their locales (Cataño, D.C., Jackson, and Miami). The other grantees, each with less-developed organizational linkages, made weaker progress toward implementation, at least in part because members did not agree on the vision or did not pool their resources to implement it.

- *Dimension 3: level of development and implementation of plans for systemic changes in policy.* Three of the grantees, those in Cataño, D.C., and Jackson, made progress toward policy changes and/or toward expanding policy influence. The collaborative in Miami-Dade did not see its work in terms of systemic change and did not move deliberately toward ensuring district-wide support of changes to policies outside. Four grantees—Charlotte, Denver, San Antonio, and Santa Ana—were at the planning stages of policy development.

- *Dimension 4: level of independence achieved by the collaborative.* Cataño and D.C. took significant steps toward sustaining the collaborative and its CERI focus through a combination of opportunistic and deliberate actions. Santa Ana also made steps to bring in significant grant funding, but this was directed toward other initiatives. Others were in the planning stages or had perhaps drawn in some minor funding supports.

- *Dimension 5: level of change in student outcomes as a result of collaborative actions.* Very little improvement on student achievement that could be attributed to the grantees was made across most sites. Jackson, Miami, and Santa Ana, however, might be credited with some test successes. Cataño might be credited with increasing the percentage of children staying in school through the middle school years. Test scores there, however, did not paint a consistent picture of progress. On the other hand, interim organizational results were evident across more sites but depended greatly on the action plans and conditions there.

In answer to the second question concerning lessons from this effort, much of the difference in progress could be traced to contextual issues and the difficulties of creating collaboratives themselves. Our analysis found that significant time and attention combined with other factors are required to build the levels of trust needed for collaboratives to function. Other factors that proved to be important were

- the inclusion of stakeholders relevant to the local context and to the collaborative's goals;
- the delicate balance of the school districts' role in the collaborative;
- the perceived legitimacy of the lead organization;
- the nature of how collaborative members work together;
- the ability to match goals to the local context and adeptly use information to inform theories of action and activities;
- the style of leadership at every stage of the collaborative's development;
- the attention to fostering the legitimacy and reputation of the collaborative over time;
- the willingness to continuously reflect on work and use data to alter strategies as necessary; and
- early attention to strategies around sustaining the *collaborative* as well as the *reform* agenda.

Observations on Improving Efforts at Collaborative Building

Other lessons were gained from review of the relationship between the funder and the sites and their initial communications about goals. Because this was a developmental effort, change and evolution might be expected. Several factors contributed to a slow start for some sites that could have been avoided with better planning. Given the formative nature of the research, we tentatively offer the following observations to funders of similar efforts in the future.

- Greater clarity of the goals and objectives in the very early stages might promote greater progress. Until the second year of our evaluation, goals were not clarified enough for all parties to understand the expectations of the foundation. Strong planning, coordination among foundation staff, and communication of expectations could provide a solid base for starting any new initiatives.
- The planning year for the sites could be made more useful by providing technical assistance. Several sites could have benefited at an earlier stage from the strategic planning offered by the technical assistance provider and with the use of data for diagnosis of problems, strategic planning, development of activities, and feedback. Early technical assistance from the planning year onward might assist sites to develop this capacity.
- Funders might consider requiring more specific types of reporting from sites. We found that sites' reliance on the evaluator for this information precluded them from developing their own capacity to collect and utilize data. Importantly, records of which teachers, principals, or parents participated in activities would be helpful in tracking effects.
- Sites did not move easily toward sustainment and systemic policy agendas, and our broader experience tells us that this is not unusual. Several fell into a typical grantee role of short-term dependency. A more hands-on approach by the funder might preclude this happening to such an extent. For example, clear

communication about the pitfalls of this approach as well as guidance in developing alternative approaches might help.

- Convenings and data-sharing were useful to sites because they helped sites learn about progress in general and their progress vis-à-vis others. This might be made a regular and routine part of an effort.

In answer to our final question, it is clear the foundation efforts produced several functioning collaboratives. Therefore, we conclude that collaboratives can be deliberately created with support. Adopting the above suggestions might not guarantee stronger progress but could reduce some of the hurdles faced by the sites in this study. While in some sites, progress was made and some promising collaboratives developed, none reached the final outcomes that the funder desired. As we have shown in this report, collaborative building is a long, arduous process, but one with at least some significant promise for improving our schools.

Collaborative Context

This appendix contains information on the sites in alphabetical order. Each section contains a description of the context at each site, a diagram showing the changes in partners over time, and one showing changes in activities.

Cataño Puerto Rico: Alianza Metropolitana de San Juan Para La Educación (AMSJE)

Commonwealth Context

Students who attend public schools in Puerto Rico tend to come from high-poverty households. In fact, all public schools in Puerto Rico are Title I schools. College-going rates for graduates from public schools in the commonwealth are very low. Standardized test scores, too, are low but from year to year vary so widely across and within schools that the instruments used to measure student performance are thought to be unreliable. Moreover, compared to students in the rest of the United States, Puerto Rican students spend very little time in school in part because of numerous scheduled vacations and the lack of a system that provides coverage for absent teachers.

Education reform efforts are moving in the direction of decentralization. In 1999–2000, each school in Puerto Rico was on the path to becoming the equivalent of a charter school with increased school-level autonomy and responsibility. Administrative roles for district superintendents and other staff were diminishing. In time, many district staff were moved into administrative positions in schools. Principals' duties were expanded to include many of the functions formerly performed by the district.

Just prior to the gubernatorial election in November 2000, the government also announced a reduction-in-force initiative in which government employees, including school staff, were given a window of opportunity to retire with increased benefits. Hundreds of principals across the island opted to retire both to take advantage of the new benefits and out of dissatisfaction with increasing responsibilities. An unusually high number of teachers also chose to retire. Because commonwealth law freezes hiring during election years, school staff who retired could not be replaced for at least a year. Thus, the island began experiencing a significant shortage of principals and teachers, leaving many positions vacant for one to two years. The opposition party gained control of the government during the elections and soon after revealed severe budget shortfalls within the Department of Education.

City Context

Cataño is a rather stable city, without much movement in or out. Part of the stability in Cataño stems from the community's relative isolation. The city faces high levels of poverty and unemployment. Many families live in low-income housing projects and are dependent on public assistance. Poverty in Cataño is entrenched. It is not uncommon to find families that have been dependent on welfare and food stamps for generations. Crime rates in Cataño are high, as are levels of violence, drug use, and alcoholism. The city government is making some efforts to attract tourism by renovating waterfront properties, such as a boardwalk.

District Context

Eleven schools make up the Cataño school district and constitute a feeder pattern. Students enrolled in Cataño's public schools are predominantly from poor families (90 percent from below the poverty level). Dropout rates and attendance problems are extremely high in Cataño and relatively few students in the elementary schools go on to high school or even middle school. The parents of Cataño students tend to have low levels of literacy. Many are dropouts themselves. Teen pregnancy rates are very high; a number of students come from single-parent homes.

The school facilities in Cataño are lacking. There are no playgrounds or athletic facilities. Noise levels in the streets around schools are high and affect the classroom environment. The high levels of pollution in the community also affect the schools. Not only are there school closings caused by high gas emissions, the district sees high rates of asthma and student absences due to respiratory illnesses.

As a result of the commonwealth's and Puerto Rico Department of Education's efforts at educational reform, schools in Cataño have experienced turmoil and unusually high administrative and teacher turnover. Moreover, tensions and turf battles have been observed as leadership roles and responsibilities in the district and within schools have been revamped and redefined. Between the 1999–2000 and the 2001–2002 school years, several personnel changes occurred, and a new superintendent was named. In eight of the eleven schools in the district, veteran principals either retired or were promoted to positions within the commonwealth Department of Education. In addition, several teachers from each school elected to retire.

AMSJE's partners are listed in Table A.1, and its goals and activities can be found in Table A.2.

Table A.1
AMSJE Partners in Year 1 and Year 4 of CERI

AMSJE Partners: Year 1	AMSJE Partners: Year 4
University of the Sacred Heart	University of the Sacred Heart
The College Board	The College Board
ASPIRA	ASPIRA
IREI	IREI
Superintendent of Cataño Schools	Superintendent of Cataño Schools
Puerto Rico Department of Education	Puerto Rico Department of Education

Table A.2
Goals and Activities of AMSJE over Four Years

	Year 1 1999–2000	Year 3 2001–2002	Year 4 2002–2003
Goal: Improve parental and school support for educational reform	x	x	x
ASPIRA parent workshops	x	x	x
ASPIRA family mentoring program			x
Goal: Nurture school leadership	x	x	x
Principals' Institute	x	x	
Monthly Principals' Council meetings			x
Goal: Implement professional development activities designed to improve teaching quality	x	x	x
Teacher workshops	x		
Mini-internships for the purpose of supporting teacher visits to other schools	x	x	
Mission and Vision workshops	x	x	
Master's degree program	x	x	x
Project SED (Seminar for the Enrichment of Teaching)		x	x
Goal: Institute a system of standardized assessments and help teachers and schools use the results for data-driven decisionmaking and planning	x	x	x
College Board assessments	x	x	x
Goal: Crystallize the experience gained in Cataño into a model of educational reform that can be promoted by the Department of Education islandwide		x	x
Goal: Begin a "scale-up" process in Cataño in which the school and the community become self-sufficient in maintaining the reform process		x	x

Charlotte, North Carolina: West Mecklenburg—Collaborating for Education Reform

State Context

Under former Governor James B. Hunt, the state set in motion a plan to become a national leader in education by 2010. The plan included an early childhood initiative; the Excellent Schools Act of 1997; the end of social promotion; significant remediation for underachieving students; and a dropout prevention law. The state's education reform agenda did not change dramatically with Governor Mike Easley's entrance in 2000. Making education a top priority of his administration, he reduced class sizes in grades K–3 and implemented character education programs and school accountability report cards in public schools. He also initiated North Carolina's first statewide pre-K program called More at Four. Over the years, however, the state faced a shrinking budget. Among other decisions, it cut professional development funds. Finally, the assessment system was audited to ensure its soundness. Some people believed that the scores for proficiency were set too low resulting in an unexpectedly high passing rate in elementary and middle schools. In addition, the state board voted to eliminate three sets of tests for a savings of $1.2 million.

District Context

The Charlotte-Mecklenburg School District (CMS) is the largest school district in North Carolina. The school district is divided into six regions, each including two or more pre-K through 12 feeder patterns. The number of CMS schools totals 145, enrolling 112,458 students in all. The ethnic distribution of CMS students is as follows: 43 percent African-American; 43 percent white; 8 percent Hispanic; 4 percent Asian; and 2 percent Native American. RAND's analysis of each of the past four graduating classes found that districtwide, approximately 54 percent of freshmen graduated four years later. In 1999, it was reported that 36 percent of CMS students were eligible for FRL.

Since our first site visit to Charlotte, a change in district leadership occurred. Superintendent Eric Smith, who during his tenure had provided a stable base for reform in Charlotte-Mecklenburg, stepped down. In the 2002–2003 school year, Deputy Superintendent Pughsley took his place. As for teacher turnover, during the four CERI years, this remained a significant challenge in the district, forcing it to recruit teachers from all over the nation.

The district's desegregation plan remained the most prominent issue facing CMS over the years that RAND visited Charlotte. Ultimately, the federal appeals court supported the Potter decision to remove the desegregation busing order. The district implemented its choice plan in fall 2002. This plan resulted in some feeder pattern changes. A few new schools opened as well. The Equity Plus II program, designed to provide more resources per pupil to schools with high concentrations of at-risk children, continued under the choice plan but eligibility changed for some schools with the redistribution of students. Incentives to retain teachers at Equity Plus II schools were sustained as well.

In 2001–2002, the district adopted a new reading and language arts textbook and curriculum from Open Court. Deciding against allowing schools to choose their own textbooks was a contentious issue in 2000–2001. As of 2002–2003, the district had participated for four years in the statewide math adoption plan.

West Mecklenburg CERI Cluster Context

In our initial visit, respondents indicated that the West Mecklenburg feeder pattern had been targeted for CERI because of its relatively poor performance compared to other parts of the district and because of its negative reputation. Not only did the cluster face high teacher and principal turnover, student mobility was high as well. About 30 percent of teachers in the cluster were inexperienced and more than 50 percent of students were not achieving at grade level. Student performance in the cluster was generally below district and state averages. As for graduation rates, they were slightly lower at West Mecklenburg High School than in the rest of the district. Compared to the 36 percent of students districtwide who participated in FRL programs, 60 percent of students in the cluster did so. On the other hand, the percentage of limited English proficient students in the cluster was low compared to the district as a whole. Finally, the facilities and supplies in the West Mecklenburg schools were lacking and inadequate.

Charlotte's partners are listed in Table A.3, and West Mecklenburg's goals and activities can be found in Table A.4.

Table A.3
Charlotte Partners in Year 1 and Year 4 of CERI

Year 1	Year 4
Charlotte-Mecklenburg Schools	Charlotte-Mecklenburg Schools
UNCC College of Education	Charlotte Chamber of Commerce
Johnson C. Smith College of Elementary Education	UNCC College of Education
Central Piedmont Community College	Johnson C. Smith College of Elementary Education
Charlotte-Mecklenburg Education Foundation	Central Piedmont Community College
Public School Forum of North Carolina	Charlotte Advocates for Education (formerly the Charlotte-Mecklenburg Education Foundation)
North Carolina Education and Law Center	

Table A.4
Goals and Activities of West Mecklenburg CERI over Four Years

	Year 1 1999–2000	Year 3 2001–2002	Year 4 2002–2003
Goal: Implement High Reliability and Comer[a]	x		
Train principals in High Reliability and Comer models	x		
Goal: Improve K–12 professional development	x		
Fund principals' retreat and monthly meetings	x	x	
Fund and assist master teachers in identifying best practices	x		
Fund and assist administrators in identifying the need for best practices	x		
Goal: Improve family involvement in students' educations	x		
Send 8 to 10 parents to weekend seminars	x		
Goal: Improve public engagement	x		
Set up a CERI Web site	x		
Develop newsletters, postcards, and videos to advertise CERI	x		
Publicize success of CERI and the West Mecklenburg cluster	x		
Identify educational issues in the press	x		

Table A.4—continued

	Year 1 1999–2000	Year 3 2001–2002	Year 4 2002–2003
Goal: Improve college access	x		
Match children to needed college access services	x		
Goal: Increase teacher recruitment and retention		x	x
Develop and implement Teacher Keepers project		x	x
Support for lateral entry teachers		x	x
Mentors for new teachers		x	x
Develop Urban Fellows Program/ Implement Teachers Needing Teachers		x	x
Implement Adaptive Schools			x
Provide Cognitive Coaching training			x
Goal: Increase leader recruitment and retention		x	x
Fund tuition for leaders to earn doctorate degrees		x	
Leadership Development Council		x	x

[a]"Comer" refers to the School Development Plan, originated by Dr. James P. Comer.

Denver, Colorado: Northeast School Collaborative

State Context

When CERI first began in Denver, the state of Colorado, led by Governor Bill Owens, was increasing its involvement in education because of rising concerns about the quality of education offered in the state. The state had introduced several initiatives, including new accountability measures, efforts to align curricula to state standards, the Read to Achieve program, a small schools initiative, and support of charter schools. The accountability system and the small schools initiative had the greatest implications for CERI schools in Denver and are described in more detail below.

The cornerstone of the state accountability system was the Colorado Student Assessment Program (CSAP), which was a new statewide standards based assessment. During the 1999–2000 school year, the CSAP was administered in selected subjects at selected grade levels. By the 2000–2001 school year, it was administered in all grades third to tenth in reading, writing, and math. The CSAP was a major indicator used in determining School Report Card grades, which publicly ranked schools from A to F beginning in 2001. Children in schools graded D or below became eligible for transportation aid to transfer to other public schools. Schools receiving an F were subject to conversion into independent charter schools. Even before the accountability system was put in place, it generated a great deal of stress for teachers who feared that the grades would be used to blame them. We heard reports that teachers were leaving failing schools for this reason. This issue was particularly relevant in the Northeast cluster schools where several schools were designated "unsatisfactory" as a result of their 2001 test scores and therefore in jeopardy of takeover.

Several controversies regarding the CSAP test emerged as implementation of the Colorado accountability system began, particularly in the 2001–2002 school year. The Colorado Department of Education made mistakes in compiling CSAP scores, depriving some schools of hundreds of points, and 20 CSAP tests were thrown out because of errors in administering the tests. Two bilingual education groups were threatening to sue the state because the Spanish version of CSAP had not been updated since 1997, whereas the English version had been updated annually.

Finally, the state was implementing a small schools initiative. The Bill and Melinda Gates Foundation donated $8 million to promote small high schools in Colorado by starting new ones and transforming existing ones into smaller units. This state initiative was a major contextual factor for the Northeast cluster high school, which experienced a large effort to transform itself into three smaller schools beginning in 2001.

District Context

Throughout the four years of our study, changes at the district level had important implications for schools and the CERI work. Multiple turnovers in the superintendency—four turnovers between 1999 and 2002—were perhaps the most significant of these changes because it was the direct cause of several changes in district policy during that time. CERI had begun under a newly appointed superintendent who was known for promoting community involvement in schools. His site-based management philosophy was in stark contrast to the policies of his predecessor, who was described as autocratic and unresponsive to the community. At that time, collaborative members were excited by the potential of working with the district in a more collaborative fashion. But in spring 2000, the superintendent was asked to resign after serving only nine months because the school board felt he was lacking the leadership and management skills needed to implement the vision he had created. An interim superintendent was named for the remainder of the school year as well as the 2000–2001 school year. After a thorough search, the board named a new superintendent in spring 2001.

This rapid turnover of superintendents led to significant policy shifts—particularly in the form of decentralization and then centralization—that created frustration and confusion within schools. Some of the new policies and reforms implemented by the district included changes to the bilingual program, issuance of school report cards by the district, partnership with the Institute for Learning to train school leaders and teachers, and placing literacy coaches in every school.

Cluster Context

Initially, the Denver Collaborative included schools from two clusters: one on the Eastside of the city and one on the Westside. During the 2001–2002 school year, the collaborative narrowed its focus to a cluster of Denver's schools from the newly designated Northeast Areas and renamed itself the Northeast School Collaborative.

Court-ordered de-busing began in 1997, and as a result, the demographics in the Northeast cluster schools shifted dramatically that year. The white population decreased significantly, precipitated in part by closure of the local Air Force base. At the same time, the Hispanic population increased dramatically and the African-American population remained fairly steady at 15–20 percent. These shifts led to new and different demands on teachers and schools, particularly with regard to services for English language learners.

Cluster demographics, however, remained fairly stable from 1999 to 2003, with some increases and decreases in enrollments of individual schools. Compared to the district, the cluster schools had larger enrollments of Hispanic and African-American students, a higher proportion of English language learners, and more students eligible for FRL programs.

Two major initiatives were ongoing in the Northeast Area between 2000 and 2003: the Gates Foundation Small High Schools Initiative and the Annie E. Casey Foundation's community-building initiative. As previously mentioned, the Gates initiative was a large endeavor for the Northeast high school. The Annie E. Casey initiative aimed to strengthen families in a comprehensive community-building approach and had organized the community to address parent concerns about discipline issues at one of the Northeast middle schools.

The Northeast school's partners are listed in Table A.5, and its goals and activities can be found in Table A.6.

Table A.5
Northeast School Collaborative Members in Year 1, Year 2, and Year 3 of CERI

Year 1	Year 2	Year 3
Dean Damon	Cross City Campaign	Annie E. Casey Foundation
Denver Education Network	Denver Public Schools	Bonsies-Stanton Foundation
Denver Community College	DCTA[b]	Denver Public Schools
Denver Public Schools	LARASA	Donnell Kay Foundation
LARASA	Metro State College	Mile High Childcare
Metro State College	Northeast and Westside principals	NEDPOE[c]
Northeast and Westside principals	PEBC	Northeast Area Schools
Piton Foundation	UCD	PEBC
PEBC		UCD
Rose Foundation		
UCD[a]		

[a]UCD = University of Colorado at Denver.
[b]DCTA = Denver Classroom Teachers Association.
[c]NEDPOE = Northeast Denver Parent Organizing in Education.

Table A.6
Goals and Activities of the Northeast School Collaborative over Four Years

	Year 1 1999–2000	Year 3 2001–2002	Year 4 2002–2003
Goal: Professional Development			
Clusterwide writing prompts	x		
Professional development events	x		
Articulation meetings		x	
New teacher training		x	
School minigrants		x	
Teacher exchange program			x
Goal: Public Engagement			
Events to build community involvement			
Parent liaisons	x		
Parent trainings	x		
Trips to Pueblo, Colo., and Atlantic City, N.J.	x		
Contributions to Northeast Denver Parents Organizing in Education			x
Developing Networks of Responsibility			x
After-school network			x
Goal: Use of data			
Data team meetings	x		
Goal: Teacher recruitment and retention			
School Web sites			x
Convening deans of local colleges and universities			x
Goal: Principal leadership			
Minigrants to principals			x
Goal: Curriculum and assessments			
Literacy coach coordinator			x
Goal: Early childhood education			
Ratings for child-care providers			x
"Tune-Up" kit for Northeast parents			x

District of Columbia: DC VOICE

City Context

The District of Columbia is unique in that it does not receive state funding and therefore is financially limited to the local tax revenues and payments provided directly by the federal government. Although the city has a thriving economy downtown, many of the organizations do not contribute to the tax base because they are government agencies, religious institutions, professional associations, or other types of nonprofits. Furthermore, many of the downtown employees live in neighboring Virginia or Maryland and pay income taxes to those states. In addition, the city must assume added responsibilities typically handled by state government, such as setting standards and implementing an accountability system. A new State Education Office was instituted in 2001 to oversee responsibilities typically assigned to state governments.

The District of Columbia population has fallen in the last several decades from around 750,000 in the late 1970s to around 570,000 in 2000. For many years, the city was subject to white flight and then significant numbers of middle-class African-Americans left the city to escape growing crime rates and locate to nearby suburbs. At the turn of the century, the decrease in population began to slow as several neighborhoods experienced "gentrification" as middle- and upper-class homeowners moved back into significantly renovated properties, decreasing access to housing for low-income families.

The city government, including the city schools, has historically been plagued with accusations of mismanagement. Complaints of dangerous mismanagement led the federal government to take the unprecedented step of taking over many city functions, including the school district, during the late 1990s. The city eventually regained control of its schools in 2001.

District Context

The District of Columbia Public Schools (DCPS) serves 71,899 students, with a falling enrollment. Districtwide enrollment fell 11 percent between the 1997–1998 and 2000–2001 school years, which might have stemmed in part from the opening of 17 charter schools in the district. The vast majority of DCPS students receive FRL benefits. The students are: 85 percent African-American; 4 percent white; 9 percent Hispanic; and 2 percent other. Approximately 22 percent are Limited English proficient. Approximately 37 percent of the students in the wealthiest areas of D.C. were in private schools compared to 19 percent of those in the poorest areas of the District.

The performance of D.C.'s schools has historically and notoriously been poor. More than 70 percent of students were below grade level in reading and math in 1997. More than 40 percent—some say more than 50 percent—of students do not finish high school. After finishing high school, those going to the University of the District of Columbia generally are said to need an additional two years of remedial work before taking college courses. While these figures are real and a source of great concern, DCPS is subject to more critical review than public schools in most cities. Because it does not reside within one of the 50 states, it is ranked in all tables produced by the federal government and compared to all 50 states. Repeatedly, D.C. (the only city on the list) is shown to have among the lowest, if not the lowest, performance, in the nation on many educational indicators.

In addition to poor student achievement, DCPS has been plagued with several crises. A few examples follow. The multiple and complicated levels of governance—including the school board, financial control board, mayor, and Congress—prompted the superintendent to resign in 2000. A citywide audit in 2001 revealed a school deficit of $62.5 million and that $50 million in 2000 was spent on private school tuitions for 2,000 special education students. The District created a large turnover in school leadership by appointing 30 new principals in the 2001–2002 school year. Finally, DCPS failed to meet Title I requirements in 2002 and was at risk of losing more than $25 million a year in Title I funding if it did not become compliant within the following three years.

Cluster Context

Unlike other CERI sites, DCPS does not have clearly defined feeder patterns in all areas of the city. DC VOICE initially focused its efforts on the Shaw–Columbia Heights neighborhoods because the schools in these neighborhoods faced significant challenges in terms of student demographic and performance indicators.

Throughout DC VOICE's first four years, the collaborative members struggled with a tension of wanting to work Districtwide while also wanting to maintain a strong focus in one area of the city. The collaborative learned early that its cluster work provided DC VOICE with legitimacy because it enabled DC VOICE to be perceived as a group that was grounded in the schools and taking concrete steps to help them improve. At the same time, collaborative members were concerned that its heavy investment in teacher and parent capacity-building was having a limited and unsustainable impact. By the fourth year, the collaborative had decided to scale back its direct services to schools but maintain a minimal amount of involvement in some promising school-based activities throughout the city, thereby dissolving the collaborative's cluster focus and shifting most of the collaborative's work Districtwide.

DC VOICE's steering committee members are listed in Table A.7, and its goals and activities can be found in Table A.8.

Table A.7
DC VOICE Steering Committee Members in Year 1 and Year 4

Year 1	Year 4
American Youth Policy Forum	American Youth Policy Forum
D.C. Agenda	D.C. Agenda
NECA[a]/Teaching for Change	NECA/Teaching for Change
Washington Lawyers Committee	Washington Lawyers Committee
19 professional community members	13 professional community members
1 principal	1 principal
4 teachers	3 teachers
	2 district administrators
	3 parents/community members

[a]NECA = Network for Educators on the Americas.

Table A.8
Goals and Activities of DC VOICE over Four Years

	Year 1 1999–2000	Year 3 2001–2002	Year 4 2002–2003
Goal: Constituency Building	x	x	x
Story sharing	x	x	x
Teacher workshops on parent involvement	x		
Listening project	x		
Right Questions project	x		

Table A.8—continued

	Year 1 1999–2000	Year 3 2001–2002	Year 4 2002–2003
Seminars and book discussion	x	x	x
Monitoring of hot issues	x	x	x
Education Resource Center	x	x	x
Information dissemination (pamphlets, newsletters)		x	x
Presentations to stakeholder groups		x	x
Representation on advisory groups for District leadership			x
Goal: Professional Development	x	x	x
Teacher research course	x	x	
Technical assistance (workshops, site visits, and planning) by professional development coordinator	x	x	
Planning new teacher induction policy			x
Goal: Research and Data	x	x	x
Studies and plans related to high-quality teaching, increased student achievement, strengthening of schools, parents/community relationship, testing and achievement	x	x	x
Research mapping	x	x	

Jackson, Mississippi: Ask for More

State Context

Mississippi struggled with finance shortfalls throughout the duration of CERI. This issue seemed only to get worse over the years. During the course of RAND's site visits, the state's accountability system also was enacted. The first set of norm-referenced state tests, considered the "dry-run," was administered to students in grades two through eight in 2000–2001. The scores from the tests administered in spring of 2002 were earmarked the baseline data. School ratings based on these scores were made public in fall 2002.

District Context

The Jackson Public School (JPS) District is the largest school district in Mississippi, with a student enrollment of 31,539. The vast majority of students are African-American (96 percent). Whites comprise the remaining 4 percent. Seventy-seven percent of the enrolled students participate in the FRL program. The district is made up of 59 schools. Eighteen of the 38 elementary schools offer pre-K classes. The district faces a high student mobility problem.

Given the lack of growth in Mississippi and the shrinking tax base in Jackson itself, JPS, too, has suffered financially. Other issues that the district has faced include finding and retaining quality teachers. According to a district representative we spoke with, Mississippi's state colleges are not filling the teaching vacancies. Adding to this problem is the large number of teachers who retire each year.

The district has responded to the state's program of accountability and standards by taking its own complementary measures to improve student learning. The central office standardized its curriculum and developed a system whereby classrooms could be evaluated by an outside source. To further assist schools, in the spring of 1999, the district began officially administering its own exit tests to second, third, and sixth graders. Moreover, it added term testing last year in the third and sixth grades to enable teachers to see where their students stand throughout the school year. Finally, to ensure that certain topics and skills are taught within a certain period of time, district-developed pacing guides were made available to critical grade levels as well. The purpose behind these various efforts was to increase communication between the district and teachers.

As for the organization of JPS itself, a measure of stability finally took hold with the tenure of Superintendent Jayne Sargent, hired in 1997. In January 2002, however, she announced that she would retire at the end of her fifth term in office. A new superintendent from within the district was named.

Other noteworthy changes in the district include the significant capital improvements and renovations made in some of the Lanier Cluster schools. Additionally, taking the lead of the Lanier feeder pattern as well as other school districts, JPS officially organized itself into seven clusters of schools that each feed into a high school. Two principals from each cluster, referred to as executive principals, serve as cluster administrators. Each of the seven cluster's principals meet monthly.

Lanier Cluster Context

We found that the individual schools in the Lanier feeder pattern show little variability with respect to their demographic characteristics. Moreover, students in the Lanier cluster consistently perform below district averages.

The elementary schools tend to have higher rates of students who participate in FRL programs compared to the middle and high schools. The percentage of students on FRL drops considerably at the high school level. This is likely more a function of students at the high school level opting out of the program rather than a reflection of substantial changes in family income.

In 1999–2000 and 2000–2001 most of the Lanier cluster schools' attendance rates tended to be slightly lower than those of the district. Between the 1998–1999 and 1999–2000 school years, the numbers of teachers dropped at all school levels, but dropped more at Lanier High School. The percentage of teachers with 0–5 years of experience increased noticeably at both the elementary and middle school levels, suggesting increasing staff turnover.

Ask for More's partners are listed in Table A.9, and its goals and activities can be found in Table A.10.

Table A.9
Ask for More Partners in Year 1 and Year 4 of CERI

Year 1	Year 4
PPS[a]	PPS[a]
Human Services Agenda	The Algebra Project[a]
JPS	Human Services Agenda
Jackson State University	JPS[a]
Millsaps College	Lanier Cluster Principals[a]
The Public Education Forum	Millsaps College

[a]Most actively engaged.

Table A.10
Goals and Activities of Ask for More over Four Years

	Year 1 1999–2000	Year 3 2001–2002	Year 4 2002–2003
Goal: To improve community and school support for educational reform	x		
Site-Based Council training	x		
Parent Training Academies	x		
Minigrants to cluster schools	x		
Principals' Breakfast meetings	x		
Principals' Academy training	x		
Goal: To build a working relationship between the collaborative and cluster schools	x		
Goal: To increase community involvement in education		x	x
Monthly Partner Meetings		x	x
Workshops designed to inform parents about school choice and the process of applying to college			x
Goal: To establish better articulation across school levels		x	x
Cross-school meetings		x	
School walkthroughs		x	
Professional development for school counselors			x
Ready to Learn Fair focused on district's pre-K and K programs			x
Meetings with staff from Head Start, daycare centers, and early childhood programs to align their curricula with that of the district's pre-K and K classes			x
College Spirit Day			x
Goal: To focus professional development around reading, writing, and math		x	x
Algebra Project Training		x	x
Support for teachers to attend reading and writing conferences			x
Goal: To push data-driven decisionmaking and planning		x	x
Goal: To nurture school leadership		x	x
Principals' Council meetings		x	x

Miami, Florida: Central EXPRESS

State Context

Florida was one of the first states to implement a high-stakes accountability system. Prior to CERI in Miami, the state had developed standards by grade level, known as the Sunshine State Standards. The state had mandated teacher professional development during monthly early-release days to provide teachers with time to meet and receive training on state standards, including how to teach them. Schools were graded annually on specific criteria, such as absenteeism rates and student test results, to assess the quality of services that the school provided and to hold the school accountable for its students' success. Schools graded D and F according to the criteria were given money by the state, through their respective districts, to support enhancement efforts. Schools given grades of A also received discretionary money from the state as an incentive. The state policy further stipulated that students who attended schools given an F grade for two out of four years were eligible for vouchers to attend private schools of their choice. This part of the policy was particularly controversial and was a subject of several court cases during the first four years of Central EXPRESS.

The most significant measure of a school's success included students' performance on the Florida Comprehensive Assessment Test (FCAT). In spring 1999, the FCAT tested reading, writing, and math and was administered in grades four, five (writing), eight, and ten. By spring 2003, FCAT reading and math tests were administered in all grades three to ten. The writing component was administered only in grades four, eight, and ten. The state's increasing focus on assessments and the consequences associated with low performance were of great concern to member schools of Central EXPRESS because they all originally graded as D or F schools.

District Context

The Miami–Dade County Public Schools is the fourth largest school district in the United States. As of 1999, Miami consisted of 350 schools and 352,595 students, 86 percent of whom were minority, 59 percent of whom were eligible for FRL programs, and 58 percent of whom spoke English as a second language. The dropout rate was approximately 50 percent each year.

Miami-Dade has also experienced a great deal of growth in enrollment, particularly of immigrant children. Miami-Dade schools were severely overcrowded. Instead of building more schools, the district had increased the size of existing schools, often by adding portable classrooms. About 10,000 new students enroll in the district every year. A significant number of these students come from Latin America or the Caribbean islands. In 1998, an average of 1,340 additional limited English proficient students were enrolling in Miami-Dade schools each month.

To manage such large numbers of students, the district is divided into six regions. Many respondents reported that the central office was very bureaucratic, with several layers of oversight. A financial scandal led to a turnover in the superintendency in 2001, but this reportedly had little if no effect on schools, which were several layers removed from the top leadership of the district. Each region had a regional superintendent, but district policies became increasingly centralized over the course of our study. For example, it adopted district-wide curriculum plans in the areas of reading, math, and science.

Central Feeder Pattern Context

The Miami Central cluster of schools, which feeds into a single high school, is one of 29 feeder patterns in Miami–Dade County Public Schools. It reflected the district in many ways, but the challenges it faced were even more extreme. The area reportedly had few community resources and was perceived as having significant problems with crime and violence. The Central feeder pattern was targeted by CERI efforts in part because of the particular challenges it faced in terms of average student demographic and performance indicators.

Enrollments in the Miami Central feeder pattern had decreased while enrollments districtwide had consistently been increasing. Regardless, respondents reported that the feeder pattern schools were terribly overcrowded and portables were prevalent on all campuses. The 11 schools served approximately 14,000 students, approximately

80 percent of whom were eligible for FRL. On average, the feeder pattern schools all had substantially higher proportions of African American students (78 percent) than the district (33 percent). Many of these students were from families that had lived in the area for generations. However, the feeder pattern also had large numbers of immigrants, primarily from Haiti and Latin America. Student mobility and drop out rates were reportedly significantly higher in the feeder pattern than in the district.

Central EXPRESS's partners are listed in Table A.11, and its goals and activities can be found in Table A.12.

Table A.11
Central EXPRESS Collaborative Members in Year 1 and Year 3 of CERI

Year 1	Year 3
Billie Birnie and Associates	Billie Birnie and Associates
Central Feeder Pattern Schools	Central Feeder Pattern Schools
Education Fund	Education Fund
Education Pact, FIU[a]	Education Pact, FIU
University of Miami	University of Miami

[a]FIU = Florida International University.

Table A.12
Goals and Activities of Central EXPRESS over Four Years

	Year 1 1999–2000	Year 3 2001–2002	Year 4 2002–2003
Goal: Improve professional development	x	x	x
Instructional Leadership Academy	x		
Writing Academy	x	x	x
New Teacher Induction and Workshops	x	x	
New Teacher Coordinators	x	x	x
Math Science Resource Teacher Master's Program	x		
Urban Education Master's Degree	x		
Travel Fund	x		
School Leadership Retreat	x	x	x
Teacher Network Policy Institute		x	x
Reading Assessment Academy		x	x
Substitute Teacher Workshops		x	
Support Services Training		x	

Table A.12—continued

	Year 1 1999–2000	Year 3 2001–2002	Year 4 2002–2003
Training for front office staff		x	
Goal: Improve parent and community involvement	x	x	x
Central EXPRESS Newsletter	x	x	x
Support for PTAs and Community Involvement Specialists	x	x	
Community Council Meetings	x	x	
Parent Resource Centers	x	x	
Goal: Improve direct services to students	x	x	x
AmeriCorps Tutors	x	x	
GEAR-UP[a]	x	x	x
Colleges and Careers	x		

[a]GEAR-UP = Gaining Early Awareness and Readiness for Undergraduate Programs.

San Antonio, Texas: ACCESS

State Context

At the state level, much talk concerned the controversial system of high-stakes, standardized testing that Texas implemented in 1990. As one of the very first states to move in this direction, it was deemed a pioneer and therefore watched with interest by a variety of groups. The most recent iteration was administered in spring 2003. It was designed to be more comprehensive and difficult. Moreover, the associated stakes were higher, given that scores were tied to promotion and graduation requirements for a greater number of grade levels.

Early in our visits we also learned that Texas had moved to mandating site-based management. It stipulated that an Instructional Leadership Team, consisting of teachers, administrators, parents, students, and the members of the business community, had to be in place and functioning at every school. The state also required that Campus Improvement Plans be developed by every school. Finally, dropout rates in the state were reported as a problem, especially among minority students. In many areas, dropout rates in these populations were as high as 50 percent.

City Context

The city of San Antonio was growing rapidly and the tax base was increasing. However, the rate of growth was distributed unevenly across the city and in fact most heavily concentrated in an area of San Antonio removed from the CERI school district.

The majority of San Antonio residents are Hispanic (59 percent) and predominantly Mexican (41 percent). Whites (32 percent), African-Americans (7 percent), and Asian-Americans (2 percent) round out the rest of the population. Most of San Antonio's residents are undereducated compared to the populations of other Texas urban areas.

District Context

The San Antonio Independent School District is one of the largest in the state. The district consists of 94 schools, serving 56,505 students. Most students are Hispanic (86.5 percent) and 19 percent are classified as LEP. Many students are bilingual, and of these a good number have limited language and literacy skills in both Spanish and English. The school district enrolls high proportions of students from low-income families (90.3 percent). The entire district is eligible for Title I, so all students receive free lunches regardless of family income. Over the years, student enrollment has decreased in part because of the closure of low-income housing projects and some loss of students to magnet schools (58,000 in 1999 to 56,505 in 2002). According to the school district, its attrition rate is 44 percent. The students who graduate from high school and then go on to schools of higher education tend to enroll in two-year community colleges.

In year 1 of CERI, a new superintendent had just been hired, replacing a superintendent who had been asked to resign before her contract's end. The new superintendent's tenure reportedly brought a sense of stability to the district. Nonetheless, teacher retention was reported as becoming a serious problem in the San Antonio school district.

Compared to many school districts in Texas, San Antonio is dependent on state, rather than property tax revenues for funding, with two-thirds of its budget coming from the state. Throughout the span of CERI, San Antonio reportedly struggled with severe budget constraints. A bond issue in the amount of $126.5 million was approved by voters in May 2002.

Burbank Cluster

The Burbank High School feeder pattern is a low-income area. The community tends to be relatively stable in that many families have lived in the area for generations. Similar to district rates, the dropout rates in the Burbank cluster are high (about 50 percent). Failure rates at the high school are also very high. Only one-third of graduating seniors enroll in college. Most attend community colleges. Compared to the rest of the district, teacher turnover is not as serious an issue in the Burbank feeder pattern. Most schoolteachers have more than 10 years of experience, while less than four percent are new to teaching. Over the four years we visited San Antonio, however, we observed turnover among several school-level administrators.

The cluster's high school is not only a magnet school, it houses one of only two International Baccalaureate programs in the district.

ACCESS's partners are listed in Table A.13, and its goals and activities can be found in Table A.14.

Table A.13
ACCESS Partners in Year 1 and Year 4 of CERI

Year 1	Year 4
IDRA[a]	IDRA
MALDEF[b]	MALDEF
COPS	UTSA's K-16 Initiatives Office
UTSA's Alliance for Education	ACCD
ACCD	San Antonio Independent School District
San Antonio Independent School District	

[a]IDRA = Intercultural Development Research Association.
[b]MALDEF = Mexican American Legal Defense and Education Fund.

Table A.14
Goals and Activities of ACCESS over Four Years

	Year 1 1999–2000	Year 3 2001–2002	Year 4 2002–2003
Goal: Promote ongoing professional development	x	x	
Meetings between middle and high school instructional guides	x		
Formation of the K–16 Leadership Team	x		
K–16 Leadership Team meetings		x	
Goal: Effectively link the different levels of schools from K through higher education	x	x	
Middle school tours for elementary school students	x	x	
Meetings between middle and high school department heads	x		
Meetings between principals and instructional guides to discuss transitions	x		
Goal: Expose students to possibility of higher education	x	x	
Career Day for middle school students	x		
Transition Day for Burbank seniors who plan to attend college	x		
Adopt-a-Hallway		x	x
Visits by "role model alumni" to the high school		x	
College campus tours and information sessions for middle and high school students		x	x
Goal: Enhance the voice and role of families and community in education	x	x	
Assist middle schools with Alliance Schools grant application	x		
Assist Burbank H.S. with Education Partnership grant application	x		
Provide leadership training for cluster school representatives	x		
Provide parent leadership training		x	x
Establish parent centers		x	x

Table A.14—continued

	Year 1 1999–2000	Year 3 2001–2002	Year 4 2002–2003
Goal: Promote changes in policy and practices	x	x	
Create a plan of action for the work group in charge	x		
Draft recommendations around 3 major issues: parent involvement; relationship between counseling and tracking; district staff development		x	
Goal: Set up indicator system that measures school success (SSI)			x
Meeting among partners to discuss the SSI idea			x
Goal: Put together lessons learned on CERI effort			x
Retreats to reflect on the work it had accomplished to date			x

Santa Ana, California: Above the Mean

State Context

In the 1970s, California was regarded as one of the best states in terms of support for K–12 education and the performance of its graduates. In the intervening years, California has faced many challenges and constraints. Proposition 13 prevented localities from increasing their tax rate, thereby limiting spending of localities without expanding tax bases. California, like Texas and Florida, has experienced large influxes of immigrants from Central and South America. The students of these immigrants often live in Spanish-speaking homes that are below the poverty level. This influx of students has taxed the existing system. In addition, the sheer growth in numbers of students has led to a teacher and facilities shortage with many children being placed in crowded classrooms without highly qualified teachers. Emergency certification is commonly used in inner-city school systems as a means to get teachers into the growing number of classrooms. These and other factors have caused California to be ranked in the lowest quartile by many measures.

California began administering the SAT-9 achievement test in 1997 to students in grades two through eleven, but the tests were not necessarily aligned to the new state standards. Ninth grade promotion tests were administered in 2001 and were highly criticized because more than 50 percent of California ninth graders failed the test.

California passed a class size reduction law SB 1777 in 1996. It provided nearly $1 billion in its first year to reduce class sizes in K–3 and continued with higher levels of funding to the present. However, the influx of teachers decreased the overall experience and education levels of K–3 teachers. The problem of less experienced teachers was a larger issue for schools with the following characteristics: high percentages of low-income students, high percentages of Hispanic students and other minorities, large schools, and schools in urban areas.

In 2002, the state was hit hard financially as a result of slowdowns in the economy and decreased tourism. In January 2002, the legislature cut the education budget significantly, eliminating funding for teacher performance awards, expanded professional development programs, and site-based awards for schools.

District Context

Santa Ana Unified School District is the sixth largest district in California. With more than 4,500 employees, it is the largest employer in Santa Ana and one of Orange County's top 10 employers. The district has 2,700 teachers and 56,000 students at 33 elementary schools, eight intermediate schools, and four high schools, with one special and two continuing high school programs.[1]

Santa Ana school district faces the same issues as those faced by the state, county, and city only more so because of its location on a major pathway of immigrants into the United States. The schools are heavily overcrowded with many temporary buildings in place. Teacher turnover is 30 percent per year and between 40 and 50 per-

---

[1] Statistics are as of 2000.

cent of teachers have less than three years of experience. Students are predominately Hispanic (92 percent) and from immigrant families. More than 75 percent of students qualify for the FRL program. The students have very low English speaking proficiency; 78 percent of students are limited English proficient. Performance on past state tests has been very poor. The dropout rate is reportedly high.

Because about 70 percent of the district's funding comes from the state, it was hit hard by the state budget cuts, which led to a 10 percent budget cut in 2002. The financial shortfalls were compounded by space and land shortages. The district gains about 2,000 students per year. This equates to a need for an additional 60 to 70 classrooms per year, which was further complicated by the state class size reduction reform.

Cluster Context

Immediately prior to the CERI launch in Santa Ana, the new superintendent reorganized the district into four areas and appointed superintendents to each area. When the CERI RFP was announced to the Santa Ana Networks and the district, the district decided to focus CERI on Area II because that was its lowest-performing area and the Area II administrator was very positive about the initiative.

The Area II feeder pattern did not differ greatly from the rest of the city, although it did have slightly higher concentrations of Hispanics, greater poverty, and more gangs and crime. The cluster enrollments have increased at varying rates, but overall they have only increased at half the district rate.

Above the Mean's partners are listed in Table A.15, and its goals and activities can be found in Table A.16.

Table A.15
Above the Mean Collaborative Members in Year 1 and Year 3 of CERI

Year 1	Year 3
Santa Ana Networks	Santa Ana Networks
Santa Ana College	Santa Ana College
University of California at Irvine	University of California at Irvine
Santa Ana Unified School District	Santa Ana Unified School District

Table A.16
Goals and Activities of Above the Mean over Four Years

	Year 1 1999–2000	Year 3 2001–2002	Year 4 2002–2003
Goal: Professional Development			
Project GLAD	x	x	x
Move It Math	x		
Project Read	x	x	x
Consistency Management and Cooperative Discipline	x	x	x
Principals' Council for Area II	x	x	x
Saturday Math Academy	x	x	x
Goal: Parental Involvement			
Resource book for parents	x	x	x
Parent Council	x	x	x
Parent Institute for Quality Education	x		
Pre-K Parent Class	x		
Outreach training for parents	x		
Community representative			x
Community based summit		x	x
Training for parent promotores		x	x
Parent promotores home visits			x

Bibliography

Baker, L. M., "Promoting Success in Educational Partnerships Involving Technologies," in Proceedings of Selected Research and Development Presentations at the Convention of the Association for Educational Communications and Technology, Sponsored by the Research and Theory Division, New Orleans, La., January 13–17, 1993.

Bergstrom, A., R. Clark, T. Hogue, T. Iyechad, J. Miller, S. Mullen, D. Perkins, E. Rowe, J. Russell, V. Simon-Brown, M. Slinski, B. A. Snider, and F. Thurston, Collaboration Framework—Addressing Community Capacity, Fargo, N.D.: National Network for Collaboration, 1995.

Berman, P., P. W. Greenwood, M. W. McLaughlin, and J. A. Pincus, *Federal Programs Supporting Educational Change, Vol. IV (Abridged): A Summary of the Findings in Review,* Santa Monica, Calif.: RAND Corporation, R-1589/4-HEW, 1975.

Bodilly, S., with B. Keltner, S. W. Purnell, R. E. Reichardt, and G. L. Schuyler, *Lessons from New American Schools' Scale-Up Phase: Prospects for Bringing Designs to Multiple Schools,* Santa Monica, Calif: RAND Corporation, MR-942-NAS, 1998.

Cuban, L., "Transforming the Frog into a Prince: Effective Schools Research, Policy, and Practice at the District Level," *Harvard Educational Review,* Vol. 54, No. 2, 1984, pp. 129–151.

Daft, R., "Bureaucratic Versus Non-Bureaucratic Structure and the Process of Innovation and Change," *Research in the Sociology of Organizations,* Vol. 1, 1995, pp. 129–166.

Dluhy, M. J., *Building Coalitions in the Human Services,* Newbury Park, Calif.: Sage Publications, 1990.

Dodge, B., "School-University Partnerships and Educational Technology," *ERIC Digest,* Syracuse, N.Y.: ERIC Clearinghouse on Information Resources, June 1993.

The Ford Foundation, "Request for Proposals: Collaborating for Educational Reform Initiative," New York: Ford Foundation, 1997.

_____, "Request for Proposals: Collaborating for Educational Reform," New York: Ford Foundation, 1999.

_____, Ford Foundation Annual Report, 2001, New York: Ford Foundation, 2002.

Gitlin, A., and F. Margonis, "The Political Aspect of Reform: Teacher Resistance as Good Sense," *American Journal of Education,* Vol. 103, 1995, pp. 377–405.

Grissmer, D., A. E. Flanagan, J. H. Kawata, and S. Williamson, *Improving Student Achievement: What State NAEP Test Scores Tell Us,* Santa Monica, Calif.: RAND Corporation, MR-924-EDU, 2000.

Himmelman, A., *Communities Working Collaboratively for a Change,* 1996 Revised Edition, Minneapolis, Minn.: Arthur Turovh Himmelman, 1996.

Hogue, T., "Community Based Collaborations—Wellness Multiplied," Oregon Center for Community Leadership, 1994.

Huberman, A. M., and M. Miles, "Rethinking the Quest for School Improvement: Some Findings from the DESSI Study," *Teachers College Record,* Vol. 86, No. 1, 1984, pp. 34–54.

Iwanowsky, J., "Can Partnering Succeed? You Betcha," *Business Officer,* September 1996.

Kaganoff, T., *Collaboration, Technology, and Outsourcing Initiatives in Higher Education: A Literature Review,* Santa Monica, Calif.: RAND Corporation, MR-973, 1998.

Keith, J., *Building and Maintaining Community Coalitions on Behalf of Children, Youth, and Families: Community Coalitions in Action,* East Lansing, Mich.: National Network for Collaboration, 1993.

Lieberman, A., and M. McLaughlin, "Networks for Educational Change: Powerful and Problematic," *Phi Delta Kappan,* Vol. 73, No. 9, 1992, pp. 673–677.

Marsh, J., "Democratic Dilemmas: Joint Work, Education Politics, and Community," dissertation, Stanford, Calif.: Stanford University, 2002.

Mattessich, P., and B. Monsey, *Collaboration: What Makes It Work—A Review of Research Literature on Factors Influencing Successful Collaboration,* St. Paul, Minn.: Amherst Wilder Foundation, 1992.

Mazmanian, D. A., and P. A. Sabatier, *Implementation and Public Policy,* with a new postscript, Lanham, Md.: University Press of America, 1989.

McDonnell, L. M., and W. N. Grubb, *Education and Training for Work: The Policy Instruments and the Institutions,* Santa Monica, Calif.: RAND Corporation, R-4026-NCRVE/UCB, 1991.

McLaughlin, M. W., "Learning from Experience: Lessons from Policy Implementation," *Educational Evaluation and Policy Analysis,* Vol. 9, No. 2, 1987, pp. 171–178.

_____, "The RAND Change Agent Study Revisited: Macro Perspectives and Micro Realities," *Educational Researcher,* Vol. 19, 1991, pp. 11–16.

Melaville, A., and M. Blank, *What It Takes: Structuring Interagency Partnerships to Connect Children and Families with Comprehensive Services,* Washington, D.C.: Education and Human Services Consortium, 1991.

Pressman, J. L., and A. Wildavsky, *Implementation: How Great Expectations in Washington Are Dashed in Oakland; Or, Why It's Amazing That Federal Programs Work at All, This Being a Saga of the Economic Development Administration as Told by Two Sympathetic Observers Who Seek to Build Morals on a Foundation of Ruined Hopes,* Berkeley, Calif.: University of California Press, 1973.

School Communities That Work, Developing Effective Partnerships to Support Local Education, Providence, R.I.: Annenberg Institute for School Reform, Brown University, 2002.

Stone, C., ed., *Changing Urban Education,* Lawrence, Kan.: University of Kansas Press, 1998.

Tushnet, N. C., *A Guide to Developing Educational Partnerships,* Los Alamitos, Calif.: Southwest Regional Laboratory, October 1993.

Weatherly, R., and M. Lipsky, "Street-Level Bureaucrats and Institutional Innovation: Implementing Special-Education Reform," *Harvard Educational Review,* Vol. 47, No. 2, 1977, pp. 171–197.

Wenger, E., *Communities of Practice: Learning, Meaning, and Identity,* Cambridge, UK: Cambridge University Press, 1998.

Winer, M., and K. Ray, *Collaboration Handbook: Creating, Sustaining, and Enjoying the Journey,* Saint Paul, Minn.: Amherst H. Wilder Foundation, 1997.

Yin, R. K., *Changing Urban Bureaucracies: How New Practices Become Routinized,* Lexington, Mass.: Lexington Books, 1979.